AMY WELBORN

2020
A BOOK OF
GRACE-FILLED
DAYS

LOYOLA PRESS.
A JESUIT MINISTRY
Chicago

LOYOLA PRESS.
A JESUIT MINISTRY

3441 N. Ashland Avenue
Chicago, Illinois 60657
(800) 621-1008
www.loyolapress.com

Cover and interior design by Kathy Kikkert.

ISBN: 978-0-8294-4694-4
Library of Congress Control Number: 2019937034

Printed in the United States of America.
19 20 21 22 23 24 25 26 27 28 Bang 10 9 8 7 6 5 4 3 2 1

INTRODUCTION

Into a messy, ordinary world, he walked. He crawled first, of course—as we all did—and then on shaky legs, toddled, . . . but then he walked. Into villages, through cities, on wilderness paths, he walked. And along the way, we met him.

We were fishermen, soaked to the skin, hauling up our day's catch, hearing a voice calling us from the shore. We were tax collectors, compromised, and slowly seeing the truth about our lives. We were a woman profoundly possessed, a man chained in a graveyard, both finding something we thought we never would have: freedom.

We were covered with sores. We were blind. We knelt uncomprehending at our dead child's bedside. We were learned in our faith. We had all the answers, so we thought. We were a boy carrying a basket of bread and fish. We were a criminal, exposed and dying on a cross. We had called ourselves friends, and now we were scattered, confused, and remorseful. We were walking down the road, wondering what to do next.

In every place, at every turn, he walked into our lives. He healed with words and touch. He fed us. He told us stories. He changed our names. He invited us to come along.

And still—he walks.

Right here, with you and with me. He promised he would never leave us, and yes, Jesus keeps his promise. It's hard to see sometimes—well, most of the time. The world is busy and distracting. Our vision is limited; our sins darken our view.

But, yes, he's still here—walking with us, freeing us, healing, teaching, telling us stories, feeding us, forgiving. Still.

Living and discerning the reality of our grace-filled days takes attentiveness and purposefulness. It's like any relationship: it takes time and intention. It doesn't just happen. Using this book will, I hope and pray, be helpful to you on that score. Along the way, I'll share stories of discernment of Jesus' presence, of the struggle to keep focused on his promise, of the challenges of staying faithful to him, as well as insights from the many spiritual writers and teachers who have helped me.

It's a privilege for me to walk with you every day over the next year as we continue to journey with Jesus together, meeting him and listening to him in trust and hope. And along with the fishermen, the women at the tomb, the lepers on the road, and that little boy with the basket, we will be surprised again and again at what this man can make with the stuff of our very ordinary daily lives.

*"Therefore, stay awake! For you do not know on which day your
Lord will come."*
—MATTHEW 24:42

On the first Sunday of Advent, I get out of bed, put my feet
on the floor—and the world tilts. Just a bit. But it definitely
tilts. I experienced vertigo once years ago and attributed it to
the aftereffects of a long plane flight. But I haven't flown in
months, and when I fell asleep last night, life seemed
predictable, on track, steady. This morning, I'm not quite
sure what's going on. I'm supposed to seek God's presence in
all moments, so here it is: a reality check. I may think I'm the
one in charge of my life, but the truth is, not a day passes
that turns out the way I'd thought it would when it began.
Well, Lord, here I am. Awake.

Isaiah 2:1–5
Psalm 122:1–2,3–4,4–5,6–7,8–9
Romans 13:11–14
Matthew 24:37–44

DECEMBER 2

On that day,/ the branch of the LORD will be luster and glory.
—ISAIAH 4:2

How often do we walk into a room and wonder, *Wait a minute, what is it I came for? Why am I here? What was I looking for?* As Advent begins, we also walk into a room—the room of the rest of our lives that begins anew every day—and we're invited to ask those same questions. And in the very season of Advent itself, we hear the answer. What or whom are we waiting for? The Lord who created us and calls us forward, that's who. Sometimes waiting can be frustrating and seem like a waste of time—until something important comes along. When we know for whom we are waiting—and the promise of glory he holds—that changes everything.

Isaiah 4:2–6
Psalm 122:1–2,3–4b,4cd–5,6–7,8–9
Matthew 8:5–11

Tuesday

DECEMBER 3

• ST. FRANCIS XAVIER, PRIEST •

*Although you have hidden these things from the wise and the learned you
have revealed them to the childlike.*
—LUKE 10:21

St. Francis Xavier, the great missionary to the East, left
narratives of his evangelization efforts, many of which
centered on children. Children were particularly receptive to
Francis's outreach. They committed prayers and precepts to
memory, they enthusiastically confronted false idols, and
when Francis was overwhelmed by the numbers requesting
his care, he sent them out. Children! Children went into
homes and prayed with the sick. Children taught the faith to
those who had not yet heard. "Life is complicated," we say.
That's true. But it's also an excuse. The Lord comes to me as a
child; perhaps today I can respond to him with childlike
openness and enthusiasm.

Isaiah 11:1–10
Psalm 72:1–2,7–8,12–13,17
Luke 10:21–24

On this mountain he will destroy/ the veil that veils all peoples.
—ISAIAH 25:7

I live in a place of hills, ridges, and valleys. When your day's
journey takes you atop one height, you can sit in your car
and gaze across to the other, picking out landmarks and
tracing roadways. God is everywhere and not literally "up,"
but spiritual seekers of every age and place have sensed
closeness to the transcendent in the high places. Why is this?
There are true mountain encounters with God—we know
about those of Moses and Elijah and Jesus himself:
memorable, startling, awesome, and maybe even frightening.
But there is also the simple fact that up there from the
heights we can see more, see further, and see differently.
Perhaps, we hope, we can edge closer to the breadth of God's
vision, the wide embrace of his love.

Isaiah 25:6–10a
Psalm 23:1–3a,3b–4,5,6
Matthew 15:29–37

DECEMBER 5

The rain fell, the floods came, and the winds blew and buffeted the house.
But it did not collapse; it had been set solidly on rock.
—MATTHEW 7:25

In the midst of a winter rainstorm, a *thud* shook the house. I looked out the window and saw that, yes, a large tree had fallen, but I could see no damage other than a crumpled gutter. No real harm done, I thought. Then, minutes later, we heard steady dripping. The back of my closet told a different story: a serious, gaping hole. Sometimes my weaknesses are easy to spot. Sometimes they are more hidden. Now's the time to listen carefully, be honest, and let the Lord rebuild, leading me to a stronger place.

Isaiah 26:1–6
Psalm 118:1,8–9,19–21,25–27a
Matthew 7:21,24–27

Friday

DECEMBER 6

• ST. NICHOLAS, BISHOP •

*As Jesus passed on from there, two blind men followed him, crying out,
"Son of David, have pity on us!" When he entered the house, the blind
men approached him and Jesus said to them, "Do you believe that
I can do this?"*
—MATTHEW 9:27–28

"Do you believe that I can do this?"

Yes, Lord, I do believe.

Isaiah 29:17–24
Psalm 27:1,4,13–14
Matthew 9:27–31

⇒ 6 ⇐

"The harvest is abundant but the laborers are few."
—MATTHEW 9:38

The people of Milan called Ambrose to be their bishop. But Ambrose wasn't a baptized Christian, so he resisted that call and even ran off to hide. In the end, Ambrose discerned the Holy Spirit at work in the people's persistence. Within short order, he was initiated, ordained, and consecrated. When I'm invited or asked to get involved in an activity, that might be God's invitation. Or it might not. It may, in fact, be temptation to move away from God's vision. How can I know? Hold it all up against what's already been revealed as true and good, first of all. Discern the voice of Jesus. Then stay close. Keep listening.

Isaiah 30:19–21,23–26
Psalm 147:1–2,3–4,5–6
Matthew 9:35—10:1,5a,6–8

Sunday

DECEMBER 8

• SECOND SUNDAY OF ADVENT •

John the Baptist appeared, preaching in the desert of Judea and saying,
"Repent, for the kingdom of heaven is at hand!"
—MATTHEW 3:1

We went to Death Valley, California, once and discovered its
name to be well earned. No, we didn't die, but in early June it
was already unbearably hot. Every step evoked the contrasts
of death and life, dryness and flourishing. Today I consider
the dry, lifeless places in my own spirit. Well, despite those
persistent little "death valleys," these weeks of Advent
suggest a different way. For a strange man stalks that desert.
He has water. He speaks to us directly and holds out the
possibility of change. He announces good news: another is
coming, one who will bring life, even to a dry,
unwelcoming place.

Isaiah 11:1–10
Psalm 72:1–2,7–8,12–13,17
Romans 15:4–9
Matthew 3:1–12

⇒ 8 ⇐

• THE IMMACULATE CONCEPTION OF THE BLESSED VIRGIN MARY
(PATRONAL FEASTDAY OF THE UNITED STATES OF AMERICA) •

*The angel Gabriel was sent from God to a town of Galilee
called Nazareth.*
—LUKE 1:26

Information is everywhere; anyone can be famous; and
everyone is supposed to achieve great things. Finding my
way in this frantic culture, I am drawn again and again to the
hiddenness of Mary. Luke's Gospel doesn't begin with her;
rather, it takes us first to the temple in Jerusalem. Great and
renowned, this place was the locus of God's most powerful
presence on earth. And God certainly makes himself known
there in the lives of Elizabeth and Zechariah. But it is
someplace else—on the margins, in the life of a teenage girl
sitting in her house—that he enters the world directly. What
else is God doing in hidden places, right now?

Genesis 3:9–15,20
Psalm 98:1,2–3,3–4
Ephesians 1:3–6,11–12
Luke 1:26–38

DECEMBER 10

*"In just the same way, it is not the will of your heavenly Father that one
of these little ones be lost."*
—MATTHEW 18:14

It's sad but generally true that if I haven't taught it to
someone else, I don't remember it. The odds of forgetting are
much greater, at least. As I have taught and written for teens
and young people, and raised five children myself, over and
over I have tried to convey this message of comfort in a
demanding, even cruel world: "You're here because God
wants you to be," I say. "God made you on purpose. God
loves you. God seeks you when you're lost. God came to
earth in the form of a child—for you." I remind them,
sometimes urgently, and that's good. It means maybe I'll
remember too.

Isaiah 40:1–11
Psalm 96:1–2,3,10ac,11–12,13
Matthew 18:12–14

Jesus said to the crowds: "Come to me, all you who labor and are burdened, and I will give you rest."

—MATTHEW 11:28

There is a wonderful call-and-response nature to the Scripture readings for Mass during Advent. In the Hebrew Scriptures we hear ancient voices yearning, sorrowing, hoping—and God, through the prophets, responding. And then in the Gospels we hear another response to our calls: the comforting, healing presence of Emmanuel, God with us, right here with us, responding to our need.

Isaiah 40:25–31
Psalm 103:1–2,3–4,8,10
Matthew 11:28–30

Sing and rejoice, O daughter Zion! See, I am coming to dwell among you, says the LORD.
—ZECHARIAH 2:14

At Mass in a cathedral in Mexico, we were seated near a large reproduction of Our Lady of Guadalupe. One man knelt in the aisle on the stone floor in front of the image. Shabbily dressed, he rose only once, winced, and rolled up his trouser leg to reveal a terribly swollen calf. He rubbed it, then returned to his knees, rocking back and forth, hands folded, lips moving continually in prayer. My heart filled, and I prayed for him, for what is revealed in the mother's loving gaze: the hope for the day when that man—and all of us—would sing and rejoice, whole and healthy, joyfully in the dwelling of the Lord.

Zechariah 2:14–17 or
Revelation 11:19a; 12:1–6a,10ab
Judith 13:18bcde,19
Luke 1:26–38 or 1:39–47

I, the LORD, your God,
teach you what is for your good,
and lead you on the way you should go.
—ISAIAH 48:17

I read a book about mammoths. Specifically, about the
centuries it took to figure out what the huge bones
discovered in places as widespread as Siberia, Ohio, and
Mexico actually were. Their discoverers were unfamiliar with
elephants, and their vision of what creatures these could
possibly be was limited by their convictions about the age of
the earth. I don't have any deep interest in paleontology, but
I am interested in knowledge, learning, and changing
understanding. How is my vision limited? Is my certainty
actually blinding me? Are my assumptions closing me off
from God's wisdom? Am I ready to let the Lord teach me?

Isaiah 48:17–19
Psalm 1:1–2,3,4,6
Matthew 11:16–19

Saturday

DECEMBER 14

• ST. JOHN OF THE CROSS, PRIEST AND DOCTOR OF THE CHURCH •

In those days, like a fire there appeared the prophet Elijah
whose words were as a flaming furnace.
—SIRACH 48:1

Elijah's words were as a "flaming furnace." St. John of the Cross, whose feast we celebrate today, writes of God's presence as "lamps of fire": "In whose splendours the deep caverns of sense / Which were dark and blind with strange brightness / Give heat and light together to their Beloved!" In the corner of my living room, flames from Advent candles flicker in half darkness, and I pray. For light, for warmth, for a flame to brighten my way.

Sirach 48:1–4,9–11
Psalm 80:2ac,3b,15–16,18–19
Matthew 17:9a,10–13

⇒ 14 ⇐

As they were going off, Jesus began to speak to the crowds about John,
"What did you go out to the desert to see? A reed swayed by the wind?"
—MATTHEW 11:7

We were on the subway in Chicago on a cold day. The car
was full of characters anyway (including us Southerners who
were shocked into icicles), and then the preacher boarded.
He was old and bearded, wearing a hat with *Repent* appliquéd
on it. He carried signs; he never stopped talking and just had
a few things to say: "You think you're above everyone, but
you're not. Judgment Day will come, and you'll see. We're all
a royal family. Ain't no one better than anyone else." We
came to our stop and walked away. "A strange figure," I said,
"and hard to ignore." Perhaps, as with outspoken John the
Baptist in the desert, we weren't supposed to.

Isaiah 35:1–6a,10
Psalm 146:6–7,8–9,9–10
James 5:7–10
Matthew 11:2–11

Your ways, O LORD, make known to me;
teach me your paths.
—PSALM 25:4

Words, words, words. Words in books, articles, and on
screens. Searching, seeking knowledge, hungry for wisdom,
we devour words, ponder sentences, and pore through
books. We've all been formed by a lifetime of millions of
words. But every Advent, I'm startled once again by a single
word: God's Word. The Word uttered in and through
absolute love and truth in obscurity and poverty. Am I ready?
Am I prepared for that path, the paradoxical way of that
eternal Word made flesh, powerful love borne in human
weakness?

Numbers 24:2–7,15–17a
Psalm 25:4–5ab,6,7bc,8–9
Matthew 21:23–27

DECEMBER 17

The book of the genealogy of Jesus Christ, the son of David,
the son of Abraham.
— MATTHEW 1:1

There is a lot to love about Italian *presepios*, or nativity scenes.
They are extravagant, brilliantly colorful, and densely
populated. Surrounding the Holy Family is generally an
entire village or community arranged in homely and often
amusing ways. A farmer chasing a goose, children at play.
You might even spy contemporary figures: popes, presidents,
and pop-culture celebrities. Why is this? Perhaps it's an
expression of the truth expressed by Matthew in his
genealogy, that the history Jesus entered and reconciled is
our history. It's not an abstraction. It's this world. Our world.
And here he is, right beside us.

Genesis 49:2,8–10
Psalm 72:1–2,3–4ab,7–8,17
Matthew 1:1–17

*When Joseph awoke, he did as the angel of the Lord had commanded him
and took his wife into his home.*
—MATTHEW 1:24

What a confusing time this was for Joseph. Confusing,
confounding, and challenging. But, guided by the Lord, he
found his way and opened his life to this completely new
reality. In the midst of confusing times, remember: the Lord
loves us and desires our peace of mind and heart. Listening to
him and letting him guide us, we'll find it.

Jeremiah 23:5–8
Psalm 72:1–2,12–13,18–19
Matthew 1:18–25

Thursday

DECEMBER 19

*[A]t the hour of the incense offering, the angel of the Lord
appeared to him.*
—LUKE 1:10–11

During Advent in these days leading to Christmas, my days
and evenings are marked by familiar rituals of all kinds.
Scriptures, prayers, and music ease me into the journey of
waiting and hope. Candles glimmer from my mother's
Advent wreath. It's time to hang the wooden "O Antiphon"
crafts my sons made years ago. The lights, the recipes, the
scents of these days create a place that I know. That day in
the temple, Zechariah approached the Lord in a familiar,
sacred ritual. As the incense wafted to heaven, the
unexpected broke in. An angel appeared with astonishing
news. Like Zechariah, in the midst of the rituals, I pause. In
the midst of the familiar, is God offering something new?

Judges 13:2–7,24–25a
Psalm 71:3–4a,5–6ab,16–17
Luke 1:5–25

Coming to her, he said, "Hail, full of grace! The Lord is with you." But she was greatly troubled at what was said and pondered what sort of greeting this might be.
—LUKE 1:28–29

I am wary of using my imagination in my prayer and spiritual life, but whenever I read the infancy narratives from Luke, I can't help but picture Mary sharing her memories of this time with those who would pass them down and eventually write them. How else would we know what happened? It's a model for me as I look back at my own life: don't sugarcoat, don't pretend that there weren't tensions or questions. Be honest about the journey. Bring it all into the light.

Isaiah 7:10–14
Psalm 24:1–2,3–4ab,5–6
Luke 1:26–38

*Mary set out and traveled to the hill country in haste to a town of
Judah, where she entered the house of Zechariah and greeted Elizabeth.*
—LUKE 1:39–40

Mary and Elizabeth have listened. They've heard good news
about each other, and they bring it all into their encounter.
They rejoice in each other's sight and welcome the precious
lives that they carry. Welcoming Mary doesn't distract from
Christ. For when we welcome her, something else happens
too; like Elizabeth, we welcome the Christ she bears. In
greeting her, we offer God praise, as her cousin does, for it is
God who has done this, graciously entering creation in this
ordinary, extraordinary way.

Song of Songs 2:8–14 or Zephaniah 3:14–18a
Psalm 33:2–3,11–12,20–21
Luke 1:39–45

Grace to you and peace from God our Father and the Lord Jesus Christ.
—ROMANS 1:7

A few years ago I stopped in the Savannah Cathedral of St. John the Baptist a few days after Christmas. As did dozens of others. Tour buses unloaded their passengers to view the sprawling Christmas crèche near the sanctuary. They waited patiently in line, viewed the nativity scene, and of course, they did not just run out the door afterward. They craned their heads to study the ceiling; they gazed at the stained-glass windows. Similarly, there are many ways to share the good news of the incarnate One. We listen; we offer food; we smile; we make room. But it all starts with an open door, inviting all to encounter the glory, the beauty, the challenge, and the grace and peace of our Lord Jesus Christ.

Isaiah 7:10–14
Psalm 24:1–2,3–4,5–6 (7c,10b)
Romans 1:1–7
Matthew 1:18–24

Thus says the Lord GOD:
Lo, I am sending my messenger
to prepare the way before me;
And suddenly there will come to the temple
the LORD whom you seek,
And the messenger of the covenant whom you desire.
—MALACHI 3:1

He sets up shop at a bustling intersection. A dozen hand-lettered signs, a sound system. He starts preaching. You know what's coming: *Repent!* During Advent, we keep running into prophets. We give lip service to their strangeness and what they say about the unexpected ways of God. I wonder, though. How open am I, really, to that preacher on the corner? I can try to mentally brush him off: not my style, not my kind of spirituality. Paradoxically, that might be the clearest sign that it's time for me to listen.

Malachi 3:1–4,23–24
Psalm 25:4–5ab,8–9,10,14
Luke 1:57–66

DECEMBER 24

*In the tender compassion of our God
the dawn from on high shall break upon us,
to shine on those who dwell in darkness and the shadow of death,
and to guide our feet into the way of peace.*
—LUKE 1:78–79

The earth turns, and hour by hour the sun sets and darkness
blankets creation. Tonight, all over our planet in every
corner, people will gather. To village chapels, to suburban
churches, to great cathedrals, perhaps even to open fields
they will come, bringing the beauty and brokenness of their
lives. They gather to listen, to praise, and to be fed. They
hear the good news of God's tender compassion, and as they
listen, the darkness draws back and light dawns.

2 Samuel 7:1–5,8b–12,14a,16
Psalm 89:2–3,4–5,27,29
Luke 1:67–79

So they went in haste and found Mary and Joseph, and the infant lying in the manger.
—LUKE 2:16

I always begin my Christmas meditation by seeking out a baby. There is always a baby at Christmas Mass. He may be a newborn, swaddled at his mother's breast as she walks up to communion. She may be studying me from a parent's shoulder, or sleeping, or chewing on a fist. Her skin may be pink, light brown, or black. He may be sleeping, gurgling, or wrestling to be free from mother's firm hold. I contemplate that baby and let the truth sink in: *This was God. God did this. God loves us so much that He came to rest . . . here.* And with the angels, I sing.

VIGIL:
Isaiah 62:1–5
Psalm 89:4–5,16–17,27,29 (2a)
Acts 13:16–17,22–25
Matthew 1:1–25 or 1:18–25

NIGHT:
Isaiah 9:1–6
Psalm 96:1–2,2–3,11–12,13
Titus 2:11–14
Luke 2:1–14

DAWN:
Isaiah 62:11–12
Psalm 97:1,6,11–12
Titus 3:4–7
Luke 2:15–20

DAY:
Isaiah 52:7–10
Psalm 98:1,2–3,3–4,5–6 (3c)
Hebrews 1:1–6
John 1:1–18 or 1:1–5,9–14

Thursday

DECEMBER 26

• ST. STEPHEN, THE FIRST MARTYR •

But he, filled with the Holy Spirit, looked up intently to heaven and saw
the glory of God and Jesus standing at the right hand of God.
—ACTS 7:55

In the basement of a London row house turned convent, a
sister told us about the Tyburn martyrs executed in the wake
of the Reformation. As she pointed out relics and narrated
the story, she never stopped smiling. How odd, we might
think, to celebrate the feast of the first Christian martyr the
day after Christmas. Doesn't the sad story break the mood?
Well, if we approach this feast of Stephen with that sister's
spirit, it won't. It is a kind of serious joy—not because
injustice or evil isn't real but because we, like Stephen, keep
our eyes on the One who saves us from it all, standing at
God's right hand.

Acts 6:8–10; 7:54–59
Psalm 31:3cd–4,6,8ab,16bc and 17
Matthew 10:17–22

⇒ 26 ⇐

DECEMBER 27

What was from the beginning,
what we have heard,
what we have seen with our eyes,
what we looked upon
and touched with our hands
concerns the Word of life.
—1 JOHN 1:1

I've sometimes wondered why baby animals seem ready for independence so much sooner than humans. My answer is admittedly nonscientific. It's about why we're here in the first place: *love.* We are born helpless, and those who love and care for us teach us how to move and survive. And so, God comes to save us. Not through ideas or abstractions and not even through instinct but as one of us, helping us learn how to live in that kingdom, and learning the only way we can: in relationship, face-to-face.

1 John 1:1–4
Psalm 97:1–2,5–6,11–12
John 20:1a,2–8

This is the message that we have heard from Jesus Christ and proclaim to you: God is light, and in him there is no darkness at all.
—1 JOHN 1:5

What I so appreciate about the depth and breadth of Christian tradition is the realism of it. We're tempted to spout platitudes and hide from the difficulties of life. But what do we get? A man hanging on a cross anytime we walk into church, and the memory of innocent children slaughtered by an evil tyrant three days after Christmas. But then again, when we find ourselves stuck in darkness and fixated on what's wrong, what do we get? Light.

1 John 1:5—2:2
Psalm 124:2–3,4–5,7b–8
Matthew 2:13–18

DECEMBER 29

• THE HOLY FAMILY OF JESUS, MARY, AND JOSEPH •

Put on, as God's chosen ones, holy and beloved, heartfelt compassion,
kindness, humility, gentleness, and patience.
—COLOSSIANS 3:12

What does it mean to love—to really love? It seems to me
that from the standpoint of a person of faith, loving means
trying to see others through God's eyes. This helps me be the
person of compassion and patience Paul calls me to be,
helping me be less likely to misread, misinterpret, and even
ignore the signals that people are sending out about who
they truly are and the pain they are in. Poet Stevie Smith
wrote a poem from the perspective of a man whose lifeless
body has just washed ashore. How many of those whom I
encounter each day might be, as the poem's title indicates,
"Not Waving but Drowning"?

Sirach 3:2–6,12–14
Psalm 128:1–2,3,4–5
Colossians 3:12–21 or 3:12–17
Matthew 2:13–15,19–23

All that is in the world, sensual lust, enticement for the eyes, and a pretentious life, is not from the Father but is from the world. Yet the world and its enticement are passing away.

—1 JOHN 2:16–17

What I'd thought was the ideal house for us in our ideal neighborhood—a 1920s bungalow in the artsy neighborhood—wasn't working for us. The boys needed more room and a basketball hoop. I was loath to move for one reason: I had a vision of myself as the type of person who lived in this kind of house in this kind of neighborhood. Letting go of that might have stung a little at first, but eventually I understood. Stepping away from that superficial, worldly sense of myself challenged me to let my identity be formed in real freedom—by and for things that will never pass away.

1 John 2:12–17
Psalm 96:7–8a,8b–9,10
Luke 2:36–40

⇒ 30 ⇐

Tuesday

DECEMBER 31

• ST. SYLVESTER I, POPE •

And the Word became flesh
and made his dwelling among us,
and we saw his glory,
the glory as of the Father's only-begotten Son,
full of grace and truth.
—JOHN 1:14

We all know that dates and calendars are somewhat arbitrary and have no inherent meaning or tie to the ebb and flow of life. Yet, the end of an old year and the beginning of a new one are useful hooks for reflection. We consider what life was like this time last year. Twelve months, hundreds of days have passed. Change, disappointment, joy. Looking back and looking forward, we see mystery and the unknown. One thing is certain: Jesus is in it all, dwelling here, present in mercy and love.

1 John 2:18–21
Psalm 96:1–2,11–12,13
John 1:1–18

Wednesday
JANUARY 1
• SOLEMNITY OF MARY, THE HOLY MOTHER OF GOD •

And Mary kept all these things, reflecting on them in her heart.
—LUKE 2:19

Over the course of days, weeks, and months, Mary reflected. She pondered; she prayed about her child—this gift, this mystery. Whether we approach the beginning of a new year with joy, dread, or simply acceptance, what better model for figuring all of it out in a fruitful way do we have than Mary?

Numbers 6:22–27
Psalm 67:2–3,5,6,8 (2a)
Galatians 4:4–7
Luke 2:16–21

Let what you heard from the beginning remain in you.
—1 JOHN 2:24

How many thousands of words do I read every day? How
many new ideas have I encountered over all these (many)
decades of life? I love to learn; I'm always seeking to
understand more of the varieties of human life and
experience. Every day I'm amazed by something new. So it is
good to hear John here reminding me of the importance of
that old, solid foundation of my faith—what I heard at the
beginning even without comprehending, those words spoken
at my baptism: "I claim you for Christ our Savior by the sign
of the cross." Everything else might be forgotten, but
belonging to him is what remains.

1 John 2:22–28
Psalm 98:1,2–3ab,3cd–4
John 1:19–28

Friday
JANUARY 3

• THE MOST HOLY NAME OF JESUS •

John the Baptist saw Jesus coming toward him and said, "Behold, the Lamb of God, who takes away the sin of the world."
—JOHN 1:29

What a burden sin is. What a relief it is to realize that Jesus doesn't want me to carry it anymore. He wants me to seek mercy and let it go. He wants me to come to him.

1 John 2:29—3:6
Psalm 98:1,3cd–4,5–6
John 1:29–34

JANUARY 4

• ST. ELIZABETH ANN SETON, RELIGIOUS •

They said to him, "Rabbi" (which translated means Teacher), "where are
you staying?" He said to them, "Come, and you will see."
—JOHN 1:38–39

I was third in line at the grocery store. When the first woman
looked at her total bill, she shook her head and motioned for
the cashier to take two of the items back. The woman
between us quickly said, "Oh, put them with mine," waving
away all protestations and cheerfully making up the
difference when it was her turn. It was a gesture that hadn't
even crossed my mind, and I was humbled. Where is the
Teacher of faith, hope, and love "staying"? What do I witness
when I accept the invitation to "come and see"? I'll discover
him around every corner, right in line in front of me, once I
start paying attention.

1 John 3:7–10
Psalm 98:1,7–8,9
John 1:35–42

Sunday

JANUARY 5

• THE EPIPHANY OF THE LORD •

Having been warned in a dream not to return to Herod, they departed for
their country by another way.
—MATTHEW 2:12

Perhaps you have seen a puzzle or an optical illusion that
initially presents one image but invites you to find another
within. What happens to me is that I can see only that first
image initially. But once I detect the second image, I can't
unsee it, and it is difficult to ever find the first image again.
The Word broke into the world, God revealing himself as a
helpless child. I thought the world was about one thing, but
now, thanks to the child, I see that reality is different,
and—mercifully—I can't unsee him. His grace pervades this
creation, and nothing else looks the same.

Isaiah 60:1–6
Psalm 72:1–2,7–8,10–11,12–13
Ephesians 3:2–3a,5–6
Matthew 2:1–12

Monday

JANUARY 6

• ST. ANDRÉ BESSETTE, RELIGIOUS •

Serve the LORD with fear, and rejoice before him;
with trembling rejoice.
—PSALM 2:12

Brother André is one of my favorite types of saints: those who persistently (some might say stubbornly) followed the Lord's promptings, never disobedient to authority but still always challenging those around him to see the possibility of God's Spirit doing something new. He served his community in Quebec humbly—as porter, sacristan, and launderer. In those positions he encountered countless people in need of healing. Through his prayers to St. Joseph, many found health again. If you go to Montreal, there you will see rising above the city the massive St. Joseph's Oratory, a church that began when a simple brother listened, responded, and gave himself to serve the Lord.

1 John 3:22—4:6
Psalm 2:7bc—8,10—12a
Matthew 4:12—17,23—25

JANUARY 7

• ST. RAYMOND OF PENYAFORT, PRIEST •

In this is love: not that we have loved God, but that he loved us and sent his Son as expiation for our sins.
—1 JOHN 4:10

When it comes to the spiritual life, we tend, naturally, to focus on our end of things. How much do I love? How strong is my faith? The late writer Andre Dubus offers a corrective in "A Father's Story." In it, one of his characters says, "Belief is believing in God; faith is believing that God believes in you." It's not about ego, putting ourselves at the center. It's simply about accepting the beautiful truth that if we are here on earth, it's because God wants us to be, and responding by living in gratitude and hope.

1 John 4:7–10
Psalm 72:1–2,3–4,7–8
Mark 6:34–44

JANUARY 8

He got into the boat with them and the wind died down.
—MARK 6:51

A year or so after my husband died at the age of fifty, leaving behind two sons under the age of seven, I received an e-mail from someone in the area I sort of knew, inviting me to have coffee. We were both Catholics, writers, and members of the same parish. So we met and talked of family, Walker Percy, Pope Benedict XVI, and other Catholic matters. And then he said, simply, "The reason I wanted to meet you is that my father died when I was seven. And I just wanted you to know—they're going to be all right." What an unexpected gift of presence in the midst of a storm.

1 John 4:11–18
Psalm 72:1–2,10,12–13
Mark 6:45–52

JANUARY 9

In this way we know that we love the children of God when we love God and obey his commandments. . . . And his commandments are not burdensome.
—1 JOHN 5:2–3

My son asked me to take a walk with him in the newly fallen snow. I didn't want to go out in the cold, so I said no. He asked again. My son is sixteen, and we have no conflicts. He has a busy life, and so do I, and he rarely takes the initiative to seek my company. This was unusual. So, more out of duty than anything else, I agreed. As I reached for my boots, I heard him say under his breath, "Yes!" It was touching and humbling, and a sweet reminder of what happens when I set my own desires aside and try to obey that commandment—to love.

1 John 4:19—5:4
Psalm 72:1–2,14,15bc,17
Luke 4:14–22a

Friday

JANUARY 10

The report about him spread all the more, and great crowds assembled to listen to him and to be cured of their ailments, but he would withdraw to deserted places to pray.

—LUKE 5:15–16

The to-do list is long. The calendar for the day, next week, and this month is crazy. But even if I don't have many formal appointments, what other needs weigh on me and require my time and spiritual energy? I am tempted to never stop, to be constantly on the go. Why? Because what would everyone do without me? I am drawn up short here by Jesus. Once again. To let him love through me doesn't mean just being out and about and engaging with others. It might just also mean finding that deserted place and quieting myself to pray.

1 John 5:5–13
Psalm 147:12–13,14–15,19–20
Luke 5:12–16

JANUARY 11

Children, be on your guard against idols.
—1 JOHN 5:21

It's easy to laugh at how we were in the past. We can't believe we ever wore those clothes or did our hair that way. What was the appeal? Why were they so important? Well, there's no need to be too hard on my past self, but that sense of distance is a good reminder for me now. The aspects of today's experiences and desires that seem so vital to my happiness? They'll fade too. So perhaps I should be wary of the kind of hope I place in all these things instead of in God. Much of what I give myself over to in the end might well be nothing but idols crumbling in the dust.

1 John 5:14–21
Psalm 149:1–2,3–4,5,6a,9b
John 3:22–30

Sunday

JANUARY 12

• THE BAPTISM OF THE LORD •

_Peter proceeded to speak to those gathered in the house of Cornelius,
saying: "In truth, I see that God shows no partiality."_
—ACTS 10:34

Jesus descended into the waters of the Jordan River to meet
us. Not just me and you, but us. All of us. As I go out and
about in different situations, I have a choice. I can look at
people in line at the grocery store, those in the crowd at the
movies, the others in my office, my clients, my customers,
my neighbors, and I can see the other, they, and them—or,
like Jesus, I can meet them, open, accepting, and ready to
find a way to "us."

Isaiah 42:1–4,6–7
Psalm 29:1–2,3–4,3,9–10 (11b)
Acts 10:34–38
Matthew 3:13–17

Then they left their nets and followed him.
—MARK 1:18

The Greek word that Mark uses at the beginning of this sentence is *euthus*. It's a word that generally means "immediately" or "at once." The amazing thing is that Mark uses this word in his Gospel forty-two times—more than it's used in all the other Gospels combined. Mark's book is short, and *euthus* adds to the sense of urgency and movement. Contemplating *euthus* adds a sense of urgency to my own inner life, too—not urgency borne of anxiety and stress but rather of a kind of amazed joy. Jesus approaches; Jesus beckons. What am I waiting for? *Euthus*.

1 Samuel 1:1–8
Psalm 116:12–13,14–17,18–19
Mark 1:14–20

JANUARY 14

[Hannah] made a vow, promising: "O LORD of hosts . . . if you give
your handmaid a male child, I will give him to the LORD for as
long as he lives."
—1 SAMUEL 1:10–11

So, I was kicked out of the organ lesson. It's not that I was
commenting or signaling. I was just there in the loft during
my thirteen-year-old's lesson because I didn't have anywhere
else to go for that hour. But after a couple of weeks, his
teacher politely requested that I sit down in the church. A
parent's presence, he said, was enough to prevent a student
from really listening on his own terms to the teacher. One
more reminder, in a roundabout way, that other people aren't
our possessions. As Hannah lived out with her son Samuel,
our children and others belong to the Lord, on an individual
journey we're called to respect as, ultimately, their
own—and His.

1 Samuel 1:9–20
1 Samuel 2:1,4–5,6–7,8abcd
Mark 1:21–28

JANUARY 15

The LORD called to Samuel, who answered, "Here I am."
—1 SAMUEL 3:4

Samuel lay sleeping in the temple at Shiloh, there in front of the Ark of the Covenant. The Lord called. Samuel may have been confused as to who exactly was calling, but in the end, he understood and responded. Wherever I am, I must listen. Folding laundry, the Lord calls. At work, at an ailing parent's bedside, the Lord calls. At a gathering with friends, pulling weeds, waiting at a stoplight, the Lord calls. Wherever I move, stand, and rest, the Lord calls. What is my response?

1 Samuel 3:1–10,19–20
Psalm 40:2,5,7–8a,8b–9,10
Mark 1:29–39

JANUARY 16

A leper came to him and kneeling down begged him and said, "If you wish, you can make me clean."

—MARK 1:40

We may not carry our wounds as visibly as this leper, but we carry them nonetheless. He couldn't hide his; we might try to hide ours. But if we hide them, how can we approach the Lord honestly, humbly, begging for his healing touch?

1 Samuel 4:1–11
Psalm 44:10–11,14–15,24–25
Mark 1:40–45

Friday

JANUARY 17

• ST. ANTHONY, ABBOT •

*When Jesus saw their faith, he said to him, "Child,
your sins are forgiven."*
—MARK 2:5

I journey to Jesus, fighting the crowds, overcoming obstacles.
I know what I need; I know what the problems are. I know
what he needs to fix and where I need healing. Down
through the roof we go. And every time, upon arriving, I am
surprised. Because Jesus really knows. He knows what I truly
need, more than I know myself.

1 Samuel 8:4–7,10–22a
Psalm 89:16–17,18–19
Mark 2:1–12

Some scribes who were Pharisees saw that Jesus was eating with sinners and tax collectors and said to his disciples, "Why does he eat with tax collectors and sinners?" Jesus heard this and said to them [that], "Those who are well do not need a physician, but the sick do. I did not come to call the righteous but sinners."

—MARK 2:16–17

I pay close attention to the signs my body is giving me. I don't make regular doctor visits (thankfully, I don't need to), but when I sense something is wrong, I'm there, as I was one Christmas Eve in the ER when a faint but familiar tingling hinted of a recurrence of shingles—and it was. May I pay as close attention to the signs—no matter how faint—of spiritual sickness as well and offer them to the One who's promised healing.

1 Samuel 9:1–4,17–19; 10:1a
Psalm 21:2–3,4–5,6–7
Mark 2:13–17

Sunday

JANUARY 19

• SECOND SUNDAY IN ORDINARY TIME •

I have waited, waited for the LORD,
and he stooped toward me and heard my cry.
—PSALM 40:2

Wandering into a church, day or night, at home or abroad,
we are bound to see them. People, that is. A woman or a
man, alone. He may be sitting in a pew gazing at the crucifix.
She may be kneeling, head bowed, a hand reaching out to
touch the foot of a statue. Fellow pilgrims with burdened
hearts, each of us coming to the Lord, trusting that he will,
indeed, hear our cries.

Isaiah 49:3,5–6
Psalm 40:2,4,7–8,8–9,10 (8a,9a)
1 Corinthians 1:1–3
John 1:29–34

Likewise, no one pours new wine into old wineskins. Otherwise, the wine
will burst the skins, and both the wine and the skins are ruined. Rather,
new wine is poured into fresh wineskins.
—MARK 2:22

My teenage son is a pretty good pianist who learns quickly.
But then, every time he thinks he's mastered the thing, life
changes. His fingers struggle in places that flowed smoothly
just last week. He has to take the piece apart and start over;
yet in the process, he discovers something. By looking at it in
a new way, almost from scratch, he's now at a deeper level.

My faith is a little like that. I think I've got it figured out,
then here Jesus comes, saying something I've certainly heard
before. Can I hear it in a new way, open to the possibility of
a new, deeper understanding?

1 Samuel 15:16–23
Psalm 50:8–9,16bc–17,21,23
Mark 2:18–22

⇒ 51 ⇐

Tuesday

JANUARY 21

• ST. AGNES, VIRGIN AND MARTYR •

The LORD said to Samuel: "How long will you grieve for Saul, whom I have rejected as king of Israel? Fill your horn with oil, and be on your way."
—1 SAMUEL 16:1

Life changes. Sometimes the path is long, straight, and predictable, and that's where we're called to be. At other times, the Lord calls us to take a turn, to shift direction, to start anew. How long will I look back in sadness and regret? It's time for me to listen, trust, take a deep breath, and be on my way.

1 Samuel 16:1–13
Psalm 89:20,21–22,27–28
Mark 2:23–28

JANUARY 22

• DAY OF PRAYER FOR THE LEGAL PROTECTION OF UNBORN CHILDREN •

O God, I will sing a new song to you.
—PSALM 144:9

At the end of Mass, the celebrant had a word of thanks for the choir. "And," he added cheerfully, "thanks to our baby choir too!" That morning, as usual, the baby and toddler voices had echoed through the cathedral. I don't think anyone minded, and if they did, the celebrant's words of gratitude undoubtedly gave them food for thought. We can express our respect for life by the decisions we make, the causes we support, and the lives we live. Our merciful, faithful God loves each one of us into existence. How can we say no when God has said yes? And sometimes our echoes of God's yes are as simple as welcoming that gorgeous, raucous, full-of-life baby choir, wherever it shows up that day.

1 Samuel 17:32–33,37,40–51
Psalm 144:1b,2,9–10
Mark 3:1–6

Thursday

JANUARY 23

• ST. VINCENT, DEACON AND MARTYR • ST. MARIANNE COPE, VIRGIN •

*He had cured many and, as a result, those who had diseases were
pressing upon him to touch him.*
—MARK 3:10

St. Marianne Cope spent three decades ministering with
St. Damien to people suffering from Hansen's disease on the
isolated Hawaiian island of Molokai. At one point, not long
after Fr. Damien's death, the author Robert Louis Stevenson
spent eight days with the sisters and residents of the Molokai
colony. Part of the fruit of that visit was a short poem
Stevenson wrote about Sr. Marianne and her sisters. The
poem acknowledges the challenge to faith that seeing such a
terrible disease presents, but it ends on a note of hope: "He
sees, he shrinks. But if he gaze again, / Lo, beauty springing
from the breast of pain! / He marks the sisters on the
mournful shores; / And even a fool is silent and adores."

1 Samuel 18:6–9; 19:1–7
Psalm 56:2–3,9–10a,10b–11,12–13
Mark 3:7–12

Friday

JANUARY 24

Jesus went up the mountain and summoned those whom he wanted and they came to him.
—MARK 3:13

In a letter to his friend St. Jane de Chantal, St. Francis de Sales writes words that I need to hear quite regularly. Freedom in Christ, he notes, means you know that serving the Lord in love happens everywhere, even (or especially) when our own plans are interrupted by his summons. He writes: "A soul that has true liberty will leave its exercise [of private prayer] . . . with an equal countenance, and a heart gracious toward the importunate person who has inconvenienced her. For it is all one to her whether she serves God by meditating, or serves Him by bearing with her neighbour; both are the will of God, but the bearing with her neighbour is necessary at that time."

1 Samuel 24:3–21
Psalm 57:2,3–4,6,11
Mark 3:13–19

All who heard him were astounded and said, "Is not this the man who in Jerusalem ravaged those who call upon this name, and came here expressly to take them back in chains to the chief priests?"
—ACTS 9:21

I sometimes forget how radical Paul's conversion was, how unexpected. It's one more reminder, certainly, to never lose hope or judge other people in some final way. And what about me? Are there parts of myself that I've given up on, claiming that it's just the way I am? Are there elements of my past I believe are impossible to overcome? What do I actually believe about God's power to make something new, true, and good out of the damaged parts of my own life?

Acts 22:3–16 or 9:1–22
Psalm 117:1bc,2
Mark 16:15–18

Sunday

JANUARY 26

The LORD is my light and my salvation;
whom should I fear?
—PSALM 27:1

When my grandson was just learning to communicate,
"Uh-oh!" was one of his standby phrases. This is pretty
common for young children, but what struck me was that he
didn't utter it only when something "bad" happened.
Whenever there was any transition, such as going from one
room to the next or getting in and out of the car, he would
say, "Uh-oh!" It was cute, but I wonder if sometimes I respond
the same way to potential or real changes in life. Do I
reflexively react with the *uh-oh* of hesitation or even outright
fear? Or do I trust in the light of God's power and love and
move forward in confidence?

Isaiah 8:23—9:3
Psalm 27:1,4,13–14 (1a)
1 Corinthians 1:10–13,17
Matthew 4:12–23 or 4:12–17

Summoning them, he began to speak to them in parables.
—MARK 3:23

My homeschooled seventh grader's Spanish text included a video component. Each unit focused on a teen girl and boy from various Spanish-speaking countries. The common thread was that all of these kids were trying to get a soccer shirt autographed by their favorite player. And it never worked out—ever! It was either lost or the signature was washed out, or they arrived late. I was *so* aggravated. About fictional characters in two-minute educational videos? Pretty dumb, but yes. It just goes to show once again the power of the story, doesn't it? Jesus knew this. He knew our yearning to be a part of the story and to follow it through to the end. So he brings us into that story through parables and through the real, true story of his life.

2 Samuel 5:1–7,10
Psalm 89:20,21–22,25–26
Mark 3:22–30

JANUARY 28

*Then David, girt with a linen apron, came dancing before the
LORD with abandon.*
—2 SAMUEL 6:14

St. Thomas Aquinas was a man of questions and answers, all
borne of deep hunger and love for God. He prayed the Mass
with intense devotion, wrote beautiful hymns, and sacrificed
much to give himself wholly to God and to share with the
world the fruit of his search. King David danced before the
Lord. Thomas burrowed deep into hard questions. Both men
did so out of love for God. We might not think of Aquinas as
devotional reading, but American fiction writer Flannery
O'Connor read his work every night before she went to bed.
In *The Habit of Being* she writes, "I feel I can personally
guarantee that St. Thomas loved God because for the life of
me I cannot help loving St. Thomas."

2 Samuel 6:12b–15,17–19
Psalm 24:7,8,9,10
Mark 3:31–35

JANUARY 29

That night the LORD spoke to Nathan and said: "Go, tell my servant David, 'Thus says the LORD: Should you build me a house to dwell in?'"
—2 SAMUEL 7:4–5

The relationship between God's will and my own efforts can be a challenge to discern and keep in balance. I hear all sorts of inspirational talk about gifts and talents, about building the kingdom of God, about being cocreators with God. Then along comes the prophet Nathan with his word from the Lord. Cautionary words—not just for David about his dreams of building a temple but also for me. Are my big plans really about the Lord's will . . . or about my own?

2 Samuel 7:4–17
Psalm 89:4–5,27–28,29–30
Mark 4:1–20

JANUARY 30

Jesus said to his disciples, "Is a lamp brought in to be placed under a bushel basket or under a bed, and not to be placed on a lampstand?"
—MARK 4:21

One weeknight, we worked with a church group to prepare and serve dinner at a local shelter for women and children. There are a few permanent residents, but most are there temporarily. A few days later, at Saturday evening Mass, the lector who proclaimed the first reading was one of those permanent residents. We had shared one kind of food and light with her, and then she shared another kind of food and light—the Word of God—with us. In this Body of Christ, all are called to let the light of Jesus shine, wherever we are, in all sorts of different ways.

2 Samuel 7:18–19,24–29
Psalm 132:1–2,3–5,11,12,13–14
Mark 4:21–25

Friday

JANUARY 31

• ST. JOHN BOSCO, PRIEST •

Have mercy on me, O God, in your goodness;
in the greatness of your compassion wipe out my offense.
—PSALM 51:3

As harmful and tragic as sin is, it is striking to me how confident the psalmist is in God's mercy. Why is he unafraid? Because he trusts in God's love. It's an attitude that St. John Bosco was committed to bringing to the lives of the children he educated in nineteenth-century Italy. To an educational culture steeped in harshness and particularly skeptical of the full human potential of the poor, St. John Bosco brought the tender mercy of God. He writes, "Be quick to forgive—and do so wholeheartedly—whenever a pupil shows he is sorry. In this case forget everything."

2 Samuel 11:1–4a,5–10a,13–17
Psalm 51:3–4,5–6a,6bcd–7,10–11
Mark 4:26–34

FEBRUARY 1

Then Nathan said to David: "You are the man!"
—2 SAMUEL 12:7A

How can we see ourselves as we really are? It might just take the rhetorical trick, as Nathan uses here, of hearing our own story as if it were happening to someone else. What would we say to that person? Here, it helps David admit his sinfulness. But it can work in reverse, as well: to help us see our strengths. After all, if your friend is going through difficulties, what do you tell him or her? To give up? Despair? No, you probably encourage and point out the good. So perhaps the next time you're down on yourself, imagine it's a good friend sharing these very difficulties with you, imagine what you'd say in response—and listen to your own hopeful words.

2 Samuel 12:1–7a,10–17
Psalm 51:12–13,14–15,16–17
Mark 4:35–41

Sunday

FEBRUARY 2

• THE PRESENTATION OF THE LORD •

[M]y eyes have seen your salvation,
which you prepared in the sight of all the peoples:
a light for revelation to the Gentiles,
and glory for your people Israel.
—LUKE 2:30–32

Today is the true end of the Christmas season. It's called
Candlemas, because today we bring our candles in for a
blessing on this feast of Jesus, the light of the world. We're
modern people living in modern times, though. Why do we
still use candles in the liturgy? Perhaps because candles made
of beeswax, the preferred material for church candles, are
fruit of this natural world into which the Lord entered.
There's something else, too: candles, in giving off light, are
themselves consumed. All in all, a pretty spectacular symbol
of the self-giving sacrifice that powers the light—Jesus'
sacrifice and, if I'm his disciple, mine.

Malachi 3:1–4
Psalm 24:7,8,9,10 (10b)
Hebrews 2:14–18
Luke 2:22–40 or 2:22–32

"Let him alone and let him curse, for the LORD has told him to."
—2 SAMUEL 16:10

In this narrative, King David is being stalked and followed by Shimei, a member of Saul's family. Remember that David had succeeded Saul as king, although Shimei saw it more as "usurpation" than succession. Hence his cursing of David. Now, here's the thought-provoking part to me. I'm living in a culture in which I'm told to be confident of myself and never, ever listen to negative voices. Haters! But David's response is different. He'd be fully justified in ignoring Shimei or even, in that culture, retaliating against him. But as he says here, he won't. Perhaps every corner of life, even the parts echoing with negative voices, can be places—no matter how strange and uncomfortable—to grow.

2 Samuel 15:13–14,30; 16:5–13
Psalm 3:2–3,4–5,6–7
Mark 5:1–20

FEBRUARY 4

Gladden the soul of your servant,
for to you, O Lord, I lift up my soul.
—PSALM 86:4

It was eleven years ago this week that my fifty-year-old husband dropped to the ground from the gym treadmill and died. In the years since, I have naturally thought a lot about grief and loss. In the wake of loss, two general sets of feelings take root. First, sadness that the person is gone or that circumstances have changed. But there's also gratitude that the person existed at all. How to come out of loss whole on the other side? For me it was prayer and time working to balance out the two, so that the day comes when I am surprised to find that as strong as the sadness was, the gratitude to God is greater now. *Thank you* has finally overtaken *Why*.

2 Samuel 18:9–10,14b,24–25a,30—19:3
Psalm 86:1–2,3–4,5–6
Mark 5:21–43

FEBRUARY 5

• ST. AGATHA, VIRGIN AND MARTYR •

"Where did this man get all this? What kind of wisdom has been given
him? What mighty deeds are wrought by his hands! Is he not the
carpenter, the son of Mary, and the brother of James and Joseph and
Judas and Simon?"
—MARK 6:2–3

The teachers of the piano studio where my son studies gave
their own recital. It was startling to see and hear these young
women, whom I had only previously experienced sweetly
helping six-year-olds play "Twinkle, Twinkle, Little Star,"
intensely engage with energetic, discordant, jagged
contemporary works. It was a reminder to me, once again, of
the mystery and depth of every person I encounter. This is
especially true with Jesus. Who is this man? After all these
years, I assume that I know what he wants of me and what
he's all about. But should I rest so easy in my
assumptions, really?

2 Samuel 24:2,9–17
Psalm 32:1–2,5,6,7
Mark 6:1–6

Thursday

FEBRUARY 6

• ST. PAUL MIKI AND COMPANIONS, MARTYRS •

*In your hand are power and might;
it is yours to give grandeur and strength to all.*
—1 CHRONICLES 29:12

The facilitator of the academic quiz competition began asking a question, and words like "persecuted" and "Nagasaki" popped out. My son buzzed in before the questioner finished, confident of the answer: "Monks!" he said. Sorry, no. The answer was "Christians." After the competition, my son was puzzled. "I thought all the Japanese martyrs were monks." Not quite, I reminded him. St. Paul Miki may have been a Jesuit novice, but many of his companions, other Japanese martyrs, and most Christian martyrs through history have been laity. All baptized, all called to be open to the strength the Lord gives to witness to love.

1 Kings 2:1–4,10–12
1 Chronicles 29:10,11ab,11d–12a,12bcd
Mark 6:7–13

Herod feared John, knowing him to be a righteous and holy man, and kept him in custody. When he heard him speak he was very much perplexed, yet he liked to listen to him.
—MARK 6:20

The truth is always compelling—even when it challenges our accepted wisdom, even when it makes us uncomfortable, even when it confuses us. Herod, of course, is not a figure to emulate. His fascination with John clearly didn't go very far, either here or when it came to the fate of Jesus. Nonetheless, I can't help but think, if even Herod didn't turn his back on uncomfortable truths all the time, then I hope and pray to do the same, and more.

Sirach 47:2–11
Psalm 18:31,47,50,51
Mark 6:14–29

FEBRUARY 8

• ST. JEROME EMILIANI, PRIEST • ST. JOSEPHINE BAKHITA, VIRGIN •

In the way of your decrees I rejoice,
as much as in all riches.
—PSALM 119:14

Josephine Bakhita was born in present-day Sudan and kidnapped by slave traders at the age of nine. She was purchased by a diplomat and ended up in Italy, where she came to faith in Jesus. The Italian courts eventually declared her legally free. She joined a convent and spent the rest of her life joyfully witnessing to the power of Christ. She wrote words as cited by Pope Benedict XVI in *Spe Salvi* that never fail to move me; words that reach across centuries and radically different experiences of life on earth; words that bring me alongside St. Josephine on our shared journey: "I am definitively loved and whatever happens to me—I am awaited by this Love. And so my life is good."

1 Kings 3:4–13
Psalm 119:9,10,11,12,13,14
Mark 6:30–34

Sunday

FEBRUARY 9

• FIFTH SUNDAY IN ORDINARY TIME •

You are the light of the world.
—MATTHEW 5:14

In every community it seems there is an enthusiastic historian or archivist or genealogist. This person is the one who preserves memories and tends the most obscure historical site or quirky museum off the least beaten path. As a restless generalist with a poor memory for detail, I'm always so impressed by and grateful for these folks. What would be lost if they weren't so committed to their call to preserve and share this tiny slice of past or present life? They are using their gifts and shining their light. Sometimes when we hear Jesus' words about being light or salt, we think big: Go out and change the world! Well, there's something to that. But there's also something to focusing whatever small light I'm called to share in this present moment, right where I am.

Isaiah 58:7–10
Psalm 112:4–5,6–7,8–9 (4a)
1 Corinthians 2:1–5
Matthew 5:13–16

Monday

FEBRUARY 10

• ST. SCHOLASTICA, VIRGIN •

As they were leaving the boat, people immediately recognized him. They scurried about the surrounding country and began to bring in the sick on mats to wherever they heard he was.
—MARK 6:54–55

Here in the early morning, in the solitude, everything makes sense. God's mysteries invite rather than puzzle me. Holiness seems natural and possible. But soon enough, footsteps and voices interrupt the silence in the house. Outside, traffic builds and somewhere a siren whines. Other human beings with their distinct personalities and stubborn ways, deeply rooted problems that resist healing, life's complexity, the unexpected—are all waiting outside. Surely if the Lord's ways make sense here in the quiet, they make sense out there, too.

The wholeness that Jesus brings is not just for the simple solitude here. For he is out there amid that suffering crowd.

1 Kings 8:1–7,9–13
Psalm 132:6–7,8–10
Mark 6:53–56

Tuesday

FEBRUARY 11

• OUR LADY OF LOURDES •

My soul yearns and pines
for the courts of the LORD.
My heart and my flesh
cry out for the living God.
—PSALM 84:3

I took my children to Lourdes, where they were struck, as anyone would be, by the presence of the sick. What was striking was not only their presence but also the pride of place they were given. In any procession or prayer service, the wheelchairs were brought in first. It seems to me that the priority given to the sick at Lourdes is a visible sign of the internal reality of every pilgrim, whether they can walk or not. They remind us that we all are "the sick." We all come to Christ through Mary, crying out for the living God, because without him we are not well, not fine, not whole. Why be on the journey at all if we were?

1 Kings 8:22–23,27–30
Psalm 84:3,4,5,10,11
Mark 7:1–13

Wednesday

FEBRUARY 12

*Jesus summoned the crowd again and said to them, "Hear me, all of you,
and understand. Nothing that enters one from outside can defile that
person; but the things that come out from within are what defile."*
—MARK 7:14–15

A college campus minister once told me that those to whom
he ministered appeared to feel more guilt over breaking diets
and falling short on fitness regimes than they did about the
actual sin in their lives. Even if feeling guilty is not the issue,
what about my time, attention, and energy? Am I as
concerned about what I give to others and the good fruit I
leave behind as I am about my body, my appearance, and
simply how others perceive me?

1 Kings 10:1–10
Psalm 37:5–6,30–31,39–40
Mark 7:14–23

FEBRUARY 13

*When Solomon was old his wives had turned his heart to strange gods,
and his heart was not entirely with the LORD his God, as the heart of his
father David had been.*
—1 KINGS 11:4

Solomon, known for his wisdom for so long, succumbed to
foolishness at the end as he turned to idols. I can say he
should have known better, but it's probably more fruitful to
look at my own choices. An idol is anything I look to for
meaning and life that only God can give. What is that
meaning and life? It's that which is eternal—which can only
come from the eternal. Only God can give the life that lasts,
the life which, in all my wandering, I'm really searching for.

1 Kings 11:4–13
Psalm 106:3–4,35–36,37,40
Mark 7:24–30

Friday

FEBRUARY 14

And [immediately] the man's ears were opened, his speech impediment was
removed, and he spoke plainly. He ordered them not to tell anyone. But
the more he ordered them not to, the more they proclaimed it.
—MARK 7:35–36

I can't begin to explain Jesus' command not to spread the
word about this healing miracle. It's never straightforwardly
explained in the Gospels, although we can certainly guess.
Maybe he didn't want his ministry to be turned into a circus
or didn't want to encourage curiosity seekers. Whatever the
reason, it's clear that at times I may be confused or even
confounded by what Jesus does or calls me to do. With Jesus,
the only thing I can ever really expect is to be surprised.

1 Kings 11:29–32; 12:19
Psalm 81:10–11ab,12–13,14–15
Mark 7:31–37

FEBRUARY 15

He ordered the crowd to sit down on the ground. Then, taking the seven loaves he gave thanks, broke them, and gave them to his disciples to distribute, and they distributed them to the crowd. They also had a few fish. He said the blessing over them and ordered them distributed also. They ate and were satisfied. They picked up the fragments left over—seven baskets.

—MARK 8:6–8

We hunger, those of us gathered in this crowd. We sense emptiness; we know we are in deep need. Jesus knows too, and, filled with compassion, his heart moved with pity, he feeds us. He gives us nourishment, he fills us, and we are satisfied.

1 Kings 12:26–32; 13:33–34
Psalm 106:6–7ab,19–20,21–22
Mark 8:1–10

Instruct me, O LORD, in the way of your statutes,
that I may exactly observe them.
Give me discernment, that I may observe your law
and keep it with all my heart.
—PSALM 119:33–34

I once sent one of my sons—at his own request—to a
summer camp on cartooning. He was extremely dissatisfied
because the class emphasized nothing much more than
self-expression. My son wanted to learn technique so that
what he put on paper actually matched what he did, indeed,
want to express. That skill wasn't going to just happen
because of his good intentions. He needed to be taught. And
so do I. In this insanely complex life and world, I need the
Lord's instruction to guide my decisions and help me
authentically express and live out what I, indeed, know in my
heart is right and true.

Sirach 15:15–20
Psalm 119:1–2,4–5,17–18,33–34 (1b)
1 Corinthians 2:6–10
Matthew 5:17–37 or 5:20–22a,27–28,33–34a,37

Consider it all joy, my brothers and sisters, when you encounter various trials, for you know that the testing of your faith produces perseverance.
—JAMES 1:2–3

My young adult daughter was sure the fellow she was dating was The One. I was glad she was happy, but an odd part of me wished she would just stay content in singlehood. Why? Because if it didn't work out, she'd be heartbroken, and that part of me wanted to protect her from that risk. One of my older sons is a good writer and derives great joy from it, but there are times I wish he would just drop it. There's a lot of agony in a writer's life. Well, I've learned that what James writes here about difficulty and perseverance is true. I suppose the best I can do is pray that through their own inevitable trials, my children will learn it too.

James 1:1–11
Psalm 119:67,68,71,72,75,76
Mark 8:11–13

FEBRUARY 18

When I say, "My foot is slipping,"
your mercy, O LORD, sustains me.
When cares abound within me,
your comfort gladdens my soul.
—PSALM 94:18–19

At the end of one swing of the pendulum is scrupulosity; at the other end is complacency. With the first, we're anxious and certain that we can never please God. With the second, we've convinced ourselves that no matter what we do, we're fine and God's fine with that. A healthy spirituality lies in between the two extremes. We're conscious of sin and weakness, yes, but also confident that when we slip, God is always present, ready with mercy and comfort.

James 1:12–18
Psalm 94:12–13a,14–15,18–19
Mark 8:14–21

FEBRUARY 19

Be doers of the word and not hearers only, deluding yourselves.
—JAMES 1:22

Company is coming; time to clean the house. Exterminator's on the way; get that living room picked up. Home appraiser called; clear out the basement right now so he can find his way around. And every time, I think, "Wow, this looks great. It shouldn't take a visitor to make this happen. And from now on, it won't!" But, of course, it always does. It's much the same with my spiritual life. I should be a doer of the word from a place of free response to the gift. Maybe someday I will be. But to think I don't need a push from a rule, regulation, or precept? That would be deluding myself.

James 1:19–27
Psalm 15:2–3a,3bc–4ab,5
Mark 8:22–26

FEBRUARY 20

He began to teach them that the Son of Man must suffer greatly and be rejected by the elders, the chief priests, and the scribes, and be killed, and rise after three days. He spoke this openly. Then Peter took him aside and began to rebuke him. At this he turned around and, looking at his disciples, rebuked Peter and said, "Get behind me, Satan. You are thinking not as God does, but as human beings do."

—MARK 8:31–33

My day is filled with moments, great and (mostly) small, that cause me to ask: What will be my approach to this? What's my perspective? What's my decision? How should I think about this moment? Will I choose to face situations with the mind of the world, avoiding suffering and sacrifice—or with the mind of the Lord of love, mercy, and courage?

James 2:1–9
Psalm 34:2–3,4–5,6–7
Mark 8:27–33

So also faith of itself, if it does not have works, is dead.
—JAMES 2:17

If you have ever driven on I-65 through Alabama, you have
seen billboards for it: Ave Maria Grotto at St. Bernard's
Abbey in Cullman. Perhaps you've followed the signs, but if
not, know that Ave Maria Grotto is a remarkable
construction by the late Benedictine Brother Joseph Zoettl.
Built over decades, it's a vast panorama of famous, mostly
religious sites—from Jerusalem to Rome to the
Alamo—made completely out of found objects: stones,
shells, buttons, broken bottles, nuts, and bolts. Every time I
go see it, I am prompted to gentle, yet persistent
self-examination, a question posed by an eccentric,
determined Bavarian monk, to consider how our faith can
shape the work we're doing with the found objects of
our lives.

James 2:14–24,26
Psalm 112:1–2,3–4,5–6
Mark 8:34—9:1

⇒ 83 ⇐

FEBRUARY 22

• THE CHAIR OF ST. PETER THE APOSTLE •

Do not lord it over those assigned to you, but be examples to the flock.
—1 PETER 5:3

When I think about each of the important older people in my life, the images all seem to involve chairs. My father's preferred spot was his desk chair in his study. My mother spent her days in her comfortable chair in the corner, surrounded by books. My grandfather had his leather-covered lounger, its arms dotted with holes burned by cigars. From their chairs they observed, they gathered, they taught, and they provided a focus for the life around them. And so it is with Peter, the fisherman who answered Jesus' call. That yes that's embodied in his chair, the symbol of his authority, isn't one of lordship and control but of being a witness—an example—of boldness, honesty, and repentance.

1 Peter 5:1–4
Psalm 23:1–3a,4,5,6
Matthew 16:13–19

Bless the LORD, O my soul;
and forget not all his benefits.
—PSALM 103:2

At the end of a long day, I am committed to make time to
pray in a proper frame of mind: blessing the Lord first, with
gratitude, before I tackle my own litany of concerns. But you
know how it goes: distractions nudge and barge in, grabbing
my attention. Nine hundred years ago, St. Bernard of
Clairvaux advised Pope Eugenius on how to maintain his
spiritual focus. He writes in his *Treatise on Consideration*: "I
desire indeed that [you should] have peace from distractions,
but I do not want [you] to make peace with them."
Sometimes distractions are legitimate and are areas of life to
bring to God in prayer. But sometimes they are just . . .
distractions. Which is it tonight? Quieting my heart, blessing
the Lord, I listen and discern.

Leviticus 19:1–2,17–18
Psalm 103:1–2,3–4,8,10,12–13 (8a)
1 Corinthians 3:16–23
Matthew 5:38–48

FEBRUARY 24

As Jesus came down from the mountain with Peter, James, and John and approached the other disciples, they saw a large crowd around them and scribes arguing with them. Immediately on seeing him, the whole crowd was utterly amazed. They ran up to him and greeted him. He asked them, "What are you arguing about with them?"

—MARK 9:14–16

Down from the mountain where they have just experienced the glory of the Transfiguration, Jesus and his friends are met with a chaotic scene of suffering and confusion. People are arguing. Continuing to read the narrative, we see a father desperate about his possessed son. Life is often a perplexing mess, and here we see that right there in the mess, ready to heal, stands Jesus.

James 3:13–18
Psalm 19:8,9,10,15
Mark 9:14–29

FEBRUARY 25

But [God] bestows a greater grace; therefore, it says:

God resists the proud,
but gives grace to the humble.

So submit yourselves to God.
—JAMES 4:6–7

Blessed Solanus Casey's road to the priesthood was challenging. Language differences and academic difficulties slowed his progress. Accepted as a Capuchin, he was finally ordained, but as a "simplex" priest, not allowed to hear confessions or preach. Here's the irony. Father Solanus Casey spent most of his priestly life serving as porter, or doorman, at the friaries in which he was in residence. In that role, he was the first point of contact for thousands of people who'd come to the friars for spiritual help. He listened to them, and he prayed with them. I can't help but marvel at the unexpected, paradoxical yet perfectly shaped space that is cleared by humility.

James 4:1–10
Psalm 55:7–8,9–10a,10b–11a,23
Mark 9:30–37

Blow the trumpet in Zion! / proclaim a fast, / call an assembly;
Gather the people, / notify the congregation.
—JOEL 2:15–16

When I am tempted to focus on Lent as an individual journey, the prophet Joel sets me straight right away. It's about us, God's people, returning to him. A description of the beginning of Lent in a 1947 seventh-grade religion textbook makes the same point: "Thousands and thousands of people upon the stage of life are adjusting themselves to their roles in this drama—this drama which is real life. . . . From all parts of the world they come and from all walks of life—kings and queens, merchants and laborers, teachers and students, bankers and beggars. . . . All are quietly taking their places, for all are actors in the sublime mystery drama of our redemption." Every one of us journeying through the season, together.

Joel 2:12–18
Psalm 51:3–4,5–6ab,12–13,14,17
2 Corinthians 5:20—6:2
Matthew 6:1–6,16–18

Then he said to all, "If anyone wishes to come after me, he must deny himself and take up his cross daily and follow me."
—LUKE 9:23

How often have I looked back after I have given in to temptation great and small, looked back after a year or even just a minute, and immediately thought, *Would it really have been so hard to say no?* Or to think of it another way, *Would it really have been so hard to say yes to Jesus' invitation?* Would it really have been so hard?

Deuteronomy 30:15–20
Psalm 1:1–2,3,4,6
Luke 9:22–25

Friday

FEBRUARY 28

• FRIDAY AFTER ASH WEDNESDAY •

This, rather, is the fasting that I wish.
—ISAIAH 58:6

The two kids I still have at home go through a pretty drawn-out process of pondering their Lenten disciplines. They change their minds. They take it upon themselves to tell each other what they need to give up. That's always helpful. And they are pushed and pulled between the desires to be either too easy or too hard on themselves. Has much changed since childhood? Not really. Not for me at least. What do I want to do for Lent? It occurs to me, though, that my Lenten journey might take on a different flavor if I started with a different question. What if I started not with "What kind of fast do I want?" but "What kind of fast does God wish?"

Isaiah 58:1–9a
Psalm 51:3–4,5–6ab,18–19
Matthew 9:14–15

Jesus saw a tax collector named Levi sitting at the customs post. He said to him, "Follow me." And leaving everything behind, he got up and followed him.

—LUKE 5:27–28

The invitation from Jesus is real and continual and comes to us every day as we embark on this spiritual journey. But still, the temptation is there to hold back. Just a little. Well, when that temptation arises for me, a memory pops up. It's a memory of an older priest who spoke about liturgical seasons and Sunday Mass in a different sort of way. Instead of calling us to self-improvement through a fantastic Lent experience, he'd brusquely remind us that this well could be—and for some of us listening certainly would be—our last Lent.

Follow me.

Isaiah 58:9b–14
Psalm 86:1–2,3–4,5–6
Luke 5:27–32

He fasted for forty days and forty nights, and afterwards he was hungry. The tempter approached and said to him, "If you are the Son of God, command that these stones become loaves of bread." He said in reply, It is written:

One does not live by bread alone,
but by every word that comes
forth from the mouth of God.
—MATTHEW 4:2–4

Hungry after forty days of fasting, Jesus is met by the tempter. What is offered, like the way offered to the first human beings, is a way of pride. Notice that every response Jesus makes to the tempter is a Scripture passage. Relying on God, letting God move and speak through our lives rather than our pride, we can respond to temptation in a different way—a way that brings life, not death.

Genesis 2:7–9; 3:1–7
Psalm 51:3–4,5–6,12–13,17
Romans 5:12–19 or 5:12,17–19
Matthew 4:1–11

Let the words of my mouth and the thought of my heart find
favor before you,
O LORD, my rock and my redeemer.
—PSALM 19:15

We once toured the Federal Reserve Bank in Atlanta. At the end they give you a little plastic bag stuffed full of shredded bills. It raises the question: How can the same piece of paper have value in one form and then no value at all in another?

(Try answering that question when it comes from an eight-year-old. Try answering it for yourself.) Value is on my mind during Lent. What do I value? Why? Why is this pastime or that object so valuable to me? My hope is that in sacrificing something that I've held as valuable, I'll rediscover the true, eternal value of my real Rock, our faithful deliverer, Jesus Christ.

Leviticus 19:1–2,11–18
Psalm 19:8,9,10,15
Matthew 25:31–46

"This is how you are to pray:
Our Father who art in heaven,
hallowed be thy name."
—MATTHEW 6:9

Yes, it's the Lord's Prayer, and yes, we recite it often. That's a good thing. But Jesus' answer to his disciples' question is about more than words to memorize. He's doing what he says: teaching us *how* to pray. He's teaching us the most fruitful, faithful approach to prayer, which, as we hear in his words, involves putting God first. Well, we think, that's obvious. But is it? It might be worth asking if we really do begin prayer by acknowledging that God is God and we're not—or if our prayer time begins with letting God know all about our views about what's wrong with life and how he should fix it.

Isaiah 55:10–11
Psalm 34:4–5,6–7,16–17,18–19
Matthew 6:7–15

Wednesday
MARCH 4
• ST. CASIMIR •

[T]he people of Nineveh believed God; they proclaimed a fast and all of them, great and small, put on sackcloth.
—JONAH 3:5

Only the first week of Lent, and already I'm making excuses and rationalizing my way out of my own freely chosen Lenten disciplines. It's sadly predictable. Fortunately, I have my children around to keep me straight. For they are, without exception, thoroughly faithful. Once my then-eleven-year-old gave up television and stuck to it the entire season without (much) complaint. I was amazed. I don't think I could have been that faithful in such a big sacrifice. They're not saints, and they certainly are skilled at making excuses in other areas of life, but I'm always humbled by the way they do Lent. Chastened and maybe even hopeful, I plod on with the fast.

Jonah 3:1–10
Psalm 51:3–4,12–13,18–19
Luke 11:29–32

*Ask and it will be given to you; seek and you will find; knock and the
door will be opened to you.*
—MATTHEW 7:7

My teen son has been driving for some time now, but I can't
let go of the routine that I grabbed onto the first morning he
drove off to school all by himself. There he goes, and I dive
in: *Our Father . . . Hail Mary . . . Glory be.* Perhaps it's reached
the point of superstition; I am not sure, and won't admit one
way or the other. And yes, he has been in one (minor)
accident. But as I pray, ask, seek, and knock, what's coming
from my heart is bigger than that specific moment in time.
I'm praying for God's guidance and protection for him on
every road, in every direction. And that prayer, I trust, will
always be answered.

Esther C:12,14–16,23–25
Psalm 138:1–2ab,2cde–3,7c–8
Matthew 7:7–12

Friday

MARCH 6

Out of the depths I cry to you, O LORD;
LORD, hear my voice!
—PSALM 130:1–2

You might think that the worst moment of my life was seeing
my husband's body on an emergency-room gurney. Well, it
wasn't. The worst came a few hours later when I had to tell
his seven-year-old son that his daddy had died. *"Out of the
depths I cry to you. . . ."* Lent began a few days later, and at Ash
Wednesday Mass in his Catholic school, the boy was one of
the offertory gift bearers. Someone took a photo, and even
now, eleven years later, the crack in my heart, mostly healed,
breaks open again to see that solemn little face and sad eyes.
But then, as now, Jesus heard his voice and accompanied
him—and all of us—through suffering to a place of peace,
comfort, and, eventually, joy.

Ezekiel 18:21–28
Psalm 130:1–2,3–4,5–7a,7bc–8
Matthew 5:20–26

Saturday

MARCH 7

• ST. PERPETUA AND ST. FELICITY, MARTYRS •

Do not the pagans do the same?
—MATTHEW 5:47

My neighbors are pagans, straight up, and I don't mean that
as a slight. It's a description that they'd heartily embrace
themselves. They are also just about the nicest people I've
ever met. They are openhearted, generous to a fault, and
their children are unfailingly polite. Honestly, I'm pretty sure
they're all a lot nicer than I am. Their kindness challenges me
to dig deeper into what I mean when I claim the name of
Christian, and right here, so does Jesus himself.

Deuteronomy 26:16–19
Psalm 119:1–2,4–5,7–8
Matthew 5:43–48

Lord, it is good that we are here.
—MATTHEW 17:4

My sons served Mass on the second Sunday of Lent. Between them in the sanctuary slouched the one-hundred-year-old concelebrant, his walker in front of him. We in the congregation were of varied abilities and stages of life, none of us whole, all of us weighed down to earth, listening to a Gospel of glory: the Transfiguration. The Lord invites us to journey with him, carrying our crosses with him as we go, inching forward until we can say—as each of us gathered does in our own way, in our own time, at last, in brilliant light—*Lord, it is good that we are here.*

Genesis 12:1–4a
Psalm 33:4–5,18–19,20,22
2 Timothy 1:8b–10
Matthew 17:1–9

$\mathcal{M}onday$

MARCH 9

• ST. FRANCES OF ROME, RELIGIOUS •

Stop judging and you will not be judged. Stop condemning and you will not be condemned.
—LUKE 6:37

I've always understood Jesus' warning here as saying to us, "You just never know. A person's actions may not be ideal, but they might be better than what he could have managed yesterday, and far better than what he would have chosen years ago. You, an outsider to someone else's life, never know." When I look at decades-old photos of myself, I see a familiar face, but as I reflect on her actions and attitudes, I sometimes confront a mystery. Who was that person? Why did she make the idiotic choices she did? Because what she did then, I'd never do now. And really, if our own motivations can be such a mystery, who are we to stand in judgment of others?

Daniel 9:4b–10
Psalm 79:8,9,11,13
Luke 6:36–38

Why do you recite my statutes
and profess my covenant with your mouth,
though you hate discipline
and cast my words behind you?
—PSALM 50:16–17

Going old-school for Lent and giving up snacking, I was surprised by the fruit of it. Somehow this simple, old-fashioned discipline made the paradox of freedom in cleaving to Christ real in a way that I had forgotten. How did that work? Well, simply because when one choice was completely off-limits, a kind of spiritual space opened up in a way that renewed me. I can mutter that as a mature adult I shouldn't need an external rule to help me reach that point, but humility calls, and so—yes—it seems I still do.

Isaiah 1:10,16–20
Psalm 50:8–9,16bc–17,21,23
Matthew 23:1–12

MARCH 11

"You do not know what you are asking. Can you drink the chalice that I am going to drink?"
—MATTHEW 20:22

A lot of self-help advice, even from a spiritual perspective, invites us to boldly follow our hopes and dreams. But then we hear Jesus, who speaks not of following our hearts but of following him. Not exploring our gifts and talents but accepting the chalice he is offering. Are the two completely separate? Not necessarily, for on the one hand, the Lord beckons to us through who we are and what we can do with our time and gifts right now. But on the other hand, the disciples left everything behind for Jesus. Even, perhaps, their own hopes and dreams. Left them there in the counting house, left the nets there on the Sea of Galilee, and left their dreams of greatness there at their mother's side.

Jeremiah 18:18–20
Psalm 31:5–6,14,15–16
Matthew 20:17–28

"There was a rich man who dressed in purple garments and fine linen and dined sumptuously each day. And lying at his door was a poor man named Lazarus, covered with sores, who would gladly have eaten his fill of the scraps that fell from the rich man's table."

—LUKE 16:19–21

"I'm doing my best," I say. "I'm doing what I can."

But am I, really?

Jeremiah 17:5–10
Psalm 1:1–2,3,4,6
Luke 16:19–31

They sold Joseph to the Ishmaelites for twenty pieces of silver.
—GENESIS 37:28

During prayer, we spill out our lives to God. We seek
understanding, comfort, peace, and perhaps even answers
about the past, present, and future. The narrative of
Joseph—from slavery and prison to becoming Pharaoh's
right-hand man—frames that search in a powerful way.
There are no easy answers to why this or that event occurred
in our lives. There are no easy answers to the question, Do I
wish things had been different? For indeed, what we often
see is the truth Joseph experienced, the truth that finds its
most profound expression in the cross: God's power can draw
great good out of tragedy, human weakness, and even sin.

Genesis 37:3–4,12–13a,17b–28a
Psalm 105:16–17,18–19,20–21
Matthew 21:33–43,45–46

Saturday
MARCH 14

[H]e squandered his inheritance on a life of dissipation.
—LUKE 15:13

I listened to a radio program on Beethoven, and part of the
discussion centered on how the composer dealt with his
encroaching deafness. Once he knew what was coming, once
he knew what work would be possible for him now and in
the future, he sketched out a plan. The point was, profound
obstacles didn't deter him from using his gifts. God shares
gifts with me through his grace. Showers me with love and
mercy, as a loving Father. Sometimes I share those gifts, but
sometimes I don't. Sometimes I hoard them; other times I
squander them, misdirecting my energies. Admitting this, in
hope, I return, trusting in the Father's mercy, ready to begin
again. No excuses this time.

Micah 7:14–15,18–20
Psalm 103:1–2,3–4,9–10,11–12
Luke 15:1–3,11–32

MARCH 15

• THIRD SUNDAY OF LENT •

"Come see a man who told me everything I have done. Could he possibly
be the Christ?"
—JOHN 4:29

I come to the well, seeking. And like the Samaritan woman,
there I meet the One who tells me the truth about myself. I
discover that I am not alone in the world, not an accident,
not a piece of a machine. I am known. I am understood. This
doesn't mean I stay still, satisfied. In telling me the truth,
Jesus challenges me to do everything but sit still and
simplistically "accept myself as I am." At the well, I encounter
that mystery: I am known; I am loved; and I am beckoned to
draw closer—for more.

Exodus 17:3–7
Psalm 95:1–2,6–7,8–9
Romans 5:1–2,5–8
John 4:5–42 or 4:5–15,19b–26,39a,40–42

MARCH 16

But his servants came up and reasoned with him: "My father," they said,
"if the prophet had told you to do something extraordinary, would you
not have done it? All the more now, since he said to you,
'Wash and be clean.'"
—2 KINGS 5:13

So many aspects of this narrative ring true to me, and
awkwardly, painfully so. Naaman has gone to Elisha to be
healed of his leprosy, but once he arrives, he's offended at
every turn. Elisha doesn't even come out to see him—a
celebrated military figure! He doesn't recommend an
elaborate ritual. He tells Naaman to simply go wash in the
Jordan River seven times. And now it's my turn. I present my
wounded self to the Lord. Am I totally open to his healing,
or am I stuck at the door, full of my own ideas, expectations,
and self-regard?

2 Kings 5:1–15b or Exodus 17:1–7
Psalm 42:2,3; 43:3,4 or 95:1–2,6–7ab,7c–9
Luke 4:24–30 or John 4:5–42

Tuesday

MARCH 17

• ST. PATRICK, BISHOP •

*Peter approached Jesus and asked him, "Lord, if my brother sins against
me, how often must I forgive him? As many as seven times?" Jesus
answered, "I say to you, not seven times but seventy-seven times."*
—MATTHEW 18:21–22

Forgive over and over and over? How do we understand this
gospel call to discipleship, which seems so difficult? How is
it even possible to live this way? The saints show us. One
striking fact about St. Patrick is something simple yet
powerful: He went back. After a boyhood of enslavement by
the Celts, after escaping across the channel to safety and a
secure life of study and ministry, he heard God's call, and he
returned—to serve the very people who had held him
captive. He embodied Jesus' call to forgiveness, and he
challenges us to follow.

Daniel 3:25,34–43
Psalm 25:4–5ab,6,7bc,8,9
Matthew 18:21–35

"However, take care and be earnestly on your guard not to forget the things which your own eyes have seen, nor let them slip from your memory as long as you live, but teach them to your children and to your children's children."

—DEUTERONOMY 4:9

What have my own eyes seen? Healing. Transformation. Sacrificial love. Forgiveness. Generosity. Life from death, joy from sorrow. When the way gets difficult and the thoughts discouraging, that's the time to remember all those things. And when other people have been brought down, that's the time to share the good news of what God, indeed, has done and will do again.

Deuteronomy 4:1,5–9
Psalm 147:12–13,15–16,19–20
Matthew 5:17–19

Thursday

MARCH 19

• ST. JOSEPH, SPOUSE OF THE BLESSED VIRGIN MARY •

*When Joseph awoke, he did as the angel of the Lord had commanded him
and took his wife into his home.*
—MATTHEW 1:24

In the midst of the fast, we're invited to a feast. Even during
Lent, on a solemnity such as this, we get a break from our
Lenten disciplines, and the celebration is on. I admit that I'm
tempted to turn my nose up at this, declaring that a serious
Christian would never break the Lenten fast, right? But, oh,
there's that pride, thinking that I know better than the
church. As St. Francis de Sales said in one of his Lenten
sermons, if our fasting is to be fruitful, one of the conditions
is "never to fast through vanity but always through humility."

2 Samuel 7:4–5a,12–14a,16
Psalm 89:2–3,4–5,27,29
Romans 4:13,16–18,22
Matthew 1:16,18–21,24a or Luke 2:41–51a

One of the scribes came to Jesus and asked him, "Which is the first of all the commandments?" Jesus replied, "The first is this: Hear, O Israel!
The Lord our God is Lord alone!"
—MARK 12:28–29

You can walk on the roof of the *Duomo*, or cathedral, in Milan. I was struck by the fact that even up there, in relatively hidden places, artisans worked and left their mark. Intricate carvings of angels and natural forms marked the way in nooks and crannies. Before the tourists came, who would ever see them? The One who gave them the gift of life and creativity would, that's who. And apparently, sharing their gifts with the Lord first and alone, even if no one else ever knew about it, was enough for them. Is it enough for me?

Hosea 14:2–10
Psalm 81:6c–8a,8bc–9,10–11ab,14,17
Mark 12:28–34

Jesus addressed this parable to those who were convinced of their own righteousness and despised everyone else. "Two people went up to the temple area to pray; one was a Pharisee and the other was a tax collector."
—LUKE 18:9–10

I thank you, Lord, that my faith isn't self-satisfied, uptight, narrow, and closed-minded. I'm glad I'm not like that Pharisee. . . . Oh, wait.

Hosea 6:1–6
Psalm 51:3–4,18–19,20–21ab
Luke 18:9–14

"How were your eyes opened?"
—JOHN 9:26

In this narrative of Jesus healing the man who was blind from birth, what brings me back again and again is the lengthy description of the man's dawning understanding of who Jesus is. He regains his physical sight immediately, but that's only the beginning. What follows is a long journey of understanding, prompted every step of the way by questions, some curious, others outright hostile. Every time a different party asks this fellow who healed him, he answers with a bit more clarity until the end, when he again encounters Jesus. Finally, the man knows who Jesus is. And he knows this, thanks in part, to all the questions he has grappled with along the way.

1 Samuel 16:1b,6–7,10–13a
Psalm 23:1–3a,3b–4,5,6 (1)
Ephesians 5:8–14
John 9:1–41 or 9:1,6–9,13–17,34–38

Monday

MARCH 23

No longer shall the sound of weeping be heard there,
or the sound of crying;
No longer shall there be in it
an infant who lives but a few days,
or an old man who does not round out his full lifetime.
—ISAIAH 65:19–20

The weight of suffering in the world, past and present, is overwhelming to me. My trust is in the Lord, who promises that this world and its pain are not the end. He made us for more, and he awaits, ready for us.

Isaiah 65:17–21 or Micah 7:7–9
Psalm 30:2,4,5–6,11–12a,13b or 27:1,7–8a,8b–9abc,13–14
John 4:43–54 or 9:1–41

MARCH 24

God is our refuge and our strength,
an ever-present help in distress.
—PSALM 46:2

We were talking to a local organist, a tiny, slight, older woman. She said she'd started out playing piano, but—and here she held up her small hands, fingers spread—"I wanted to make a big sound, and it's just not possible with these fingers." So she turned to the pipe organ, where, with the help of rushing winds, she could fill a church with mighty sounds of praise with the lightest human touch. The choices I make today are only the faintest footprint in a dense, busy world. Perhaps with God's help, and dependent on his grace, I can make more of a difference than I think, and more than I can ever do in my own strength.

Ezekiel 47:1–9,12
Psalm 46:2–3,5–6,8–9
John 5:1–16

The angel Gabriel was sent from God to a town of Galilee called Nazareth, to a virgin betrothed to a man named Joseph . . . and the virgin's name was Mary.
—LUKE 1:26–27

Big things were happening around the world in the first century. Empires were rising and falling, wars being fought, great men making speeches and erecting statues in their own honor. Greatness and importance were easy to define. Books were being written to record what was worth remembering. And then there was Nazareth, a place no one cared about, and a young Jewish woman quietly doing unimportant and unmemorable things in her home. Yes, all the busy, smart people knew exactly what was most important and what it would take to change the world.

Isaiah 7:10–14; 8:10
Psalm 40:7–8,8–9,10,11 (8a, 9a)
Hebrews 10:4–10
Luke 1:26–38

Thursday

MARCH 26

I came in the name of my Father, but you do not accept me; yet if another comes in his own name, you will accept him.
—JOHN 5:43

God meets us through creation, that's true. But at the same time, we must continually discern as we encounter the Lord in this created world. Am I responding to the creature and the created, or to the Lord who is behind and above it all? Here, Jesus is challenging those who are witnessing his signs and hearing his words. Are they paying attention? Are they responding to him in a deep way through what they witness, or through something superficial instead?

Exodus 32:7–14
Psalm 106:19–20,21–22,23
John 5:31–47

Friday

MARCH 27

When the just cry out, the LORD hears them,
and from all their distress he rescues them.
—PSALM 34:18

It seemed as if every time we passed the church around the corner from our apartment in Ferrara, Italy, the door was locked. Finally, one afternoon while hunting for groceries, I noted an open door, so I peeked in: worn wood pews, an elaborate old altar. Near what had been the grill, through which cloistered sisters had heard Mass in this former Carmelite convent chapel, stood a display: photographs of one Sister Veronica, who died in 1964, now declared a Servant of God, along with a notebook filled with intercessions. *All this time*, I thought, *a saint was around the corner, hidden.* I wondered how many others there might be around other corners, behind other doors in my neighborhood—lives in which God is at work, hearing, rescuing, drawing near.

Wisdom 2:1a,12–22
Psalm 34:17–18,19–20,21,23
John 7:1–2,10,25–30

Others said, "This is the Christ." But others said, "The Christ will not come from Galilee, will he?"
—JOHN 7:41

As I move through my day, Jesus meets me in the most unexpected places. Will I be open to recognize him, no matter where or how he comes?

Jeremiah 11:18–20
Psalm 7:2–3,9bc–10,11–12
John 7:40–53

Sunday

MARCH 29

• FIFTH SUNDAY OF LENT •

And when he had said this, he cried out in a loud voice, "Lazarus, come out!" The dead man came out, tied hand and foot with burial bands, and his face was wrapped in a cloth. So Jesus said to them, "Untie him and let him go."
—JOHN 11:43–44

There is more than one kind of death, and there is more than one kind of tomb in which the dead parts of ourselves lie, dark and still. Jesus stands outside every one of those tombs. His power is stronger than the stone, stronger than any kind of death. He stands; he desires our freedom; and to each of us he calls, "Come out!"

Ezekiel 37:12–14
Psalm 130:1–2,3–4,5–6,7–8
Romans 8:8–11
John 11:1–45 or 11:3–7,17,20–27,33b–45

Jesus bent down and began to write on the ground with his finger.
—JOHN 8:6

What did he write? We don't know. Quite often in the words and actions of Jesus, we encounter mystery. It can be frustrating and curious. But what really matters is the other reality we encounter, what the woman at the center of this drama receives: mercy, and a chance to begin again.

Daniel 13:1–9,15–17,19–30,33–62 or
13:41c–62 or 2 Kings 4:18b–21,32–37
Psalm 23:1–3a,3b–4,5,6 or 17:1,6–7,8b and 15
John 8:1–11 or 11:1–45

MARCH 31

From Mount Hor the children of Israel set out on the Red Sea road, to bypass the land of Edom.
—NUMBERS 21:4

We live right behind a park that bears a long and interesting history. As we walk around the grassy areas, the pond and stream, the baseball fields, and over the hill that leads back home, we like to talk about and imagine the zoo that used to be there. We remember Miss Fancy, the elephant who regularly escaped and could be found wandering the nearby neighborhoods. Surrounded by history, we walk. During Lent, we walk in history too, in a different, invisible but real landscape. We walk with brothers and sisters, past and present, together on a journey led by the Lord—led to safety, peace, and life.

Numbers 21:4–9
Psalm 102:2–3,16–18,19–21
John 8:21–30

Wednesday
APRIL 1

Blessed are you who look into the depths
from your throne upon the cherubim;
praiseworthy and exalted above all forever.
—DANIEL 3:55

Let's count our blessings. Let's go around the table and share
what we're thankful for. Let's each thank God for what he's
done for us. Yes, let's. But then, let's do something else. Let's
say out loud what's bothering us, what's missing, what's sad,
and what's downright terrible right now. And then, as those
true words about reality echo, let's come back and bless the
Lord. Bless the One who looks into the depths—our depths.
Blessing the Lord in the midst of the mess doesn't mean we're
minimizing our pain. It's a sign of faith that God is indeed
greater than all of this, now and forever.

Daniel 3:14–20,91–92,95
Daniel 3:52,53,54,55,56
John 8:31–42

Thursday

APRIL 2

Look to the LORD in his strength;
seek to serve him constantly.
—PSALM 105:4

I had never heard of today's saint, so I looked him up.
St. Francis of Paola was a fifteenth-century reforming
Franciscan. Composer Franz Liszt was named for him and
treated him as a patron saint, even writing a piano piece
inspired by one of his miracles. After exploring all of these
connections and journeying between the psalmist, the
mendicant, and the composer, I happened upon these words
of St. Francis: "Put aside hatred and hostility. . . .
Remembering grievances works great damage. It is
accompanied by anger, fosters sin, and brings a hatred for
justice. It is a rusty arrow spreading poison in the soul." The
psalmist calls me to serve the Lord constantly, and what a
powerful way to do so, letting go of resentment and letting
mercy guide me instead.

Genesis 17:3–9
Psalm 105:4–5,6–7,8–9
John 8:51–59

In my distress I called upon the LORD
and cried out to my God;
From his temple he heard my voice,
and my cry to him reached his ears.
—PSALM 18:7

There is a religious community near us that is centered on those in recovery from substance abuse. Every year, they offer a live stations of the cross on one Friday during Lent. It is deeply moving, humbling, and hopeful to hear these women and men witness to the reality and power of Jesus' love. These aren't just words on a page or echoing in a church. This is real. The Lord really does heal. These women and men testify to that, to that grace that met them where they were—as broken as human beings can be—and brought them through, up, and out into light: resurrection.

Jeremiah 20:10–13
Psalm 18:2–3a,3bc–4,5–6,7
John 10:31–42

*I will take the children of Israel from among the nations to which they
have come, and gather them from all sides to bring them back to
their land.*
—EZEKIEL 37:21

These days I can pretty much design my life. I can select
what channels come through my television or radio. I can
direct almost everything that impacts me. There's a name for
it: curating. I can curate my own life to suit my needs and
wishes. But not this coming week. Not Holy Week. During
this week, I set aside that power to control and shape my
own life, and I join others from all over the world as we hear
faint cries and hints of a Messiah. We wonder what it all
means, we pick up our palms, and wait.

Ezekiel 37:21–28
Jeremiah 31:10,11–12abcd,13
John 11:45–56

Pilate said to them, "Then what shall I do with Jesus called Christ?"
They all said, "Let him be crucified!"
—MATTHEW 27:22

Every parish Palm Sunday procession I've been a part of
begins and ends the same way. The Gospel is proclaimed, the
music begins, and we begin our journey together. Within
minutes or even seconds, things change. We spread out,
people at the front and back are at different places in the
music, our voices falter and then fade away. It's probably
frustrating to the planners, but it's actually a good metaphor
for this week: this descent from high hopes to disarray. It's
even a metaphor for my life of faith: good intentions dashed.
Well, I'll gather myself again and ready myself for another
chance to follow and stay focused this time, because,
mercifully, there always is.

PROCESSION:
Matthew 21:1–11

MASS:
Isaiah 50:4–7
Psalm 22:8–9,17–18,19–20,23–24 (2a)
Philippians 2:6–11
Matthew 26:14—27:66 or 27:11–54

Monday

APRIL 6

• MONDAY OF HOLY WEEK •

I formed you, and set you
as a covenant for the people,
a light for the nations.
—ISAIAH 42:6

After Mass on Palm Sunday in Mexico City, almost every
person in the packed church approached the sanctuary to have
their palms blessed by the priest. Many elaborately woven
creations, including crucifixes completely woven from palm
leaves, had been purchased from craftspeople right outside the
church doors. After Mass, the people streamed out of the
church, carrying what had been blessed out into the city. What
struck me was that, as is normal there, only a small number had
received communion. But the understanding of the dynamic of
this moment clearly remained: the grace that is poured out in
this place is not for hoarding. Whether it is his life borne
within our bodies or the symbols and signs we carry in our
hands, the grace we receive is given to us to share, sharing light
with those in darkness.

Isaiah 42:1–7
Psalm 27:1,2,3,13–14
John 12:1–11

Tuesday

APRIL 7

• TUESDAY OF HOLY WEEK •

*Peter said to him, "Master, why can I not follow you now? I will lay
down my life for you." Jesus answered, "Will you lay down your life for
me? Amen, amen, I say to you, the cock will not crow before you
deny me three times."*
—JOHN 13:37–38

Sometimes by the end of Lent, we may feel as Peter felt after
this conversation with Jesus. We began with all kinds of good
intentions, but perhaps it hasn't worked out the way we'd
planned or hoped. That doesn't mean it's over. It wasn't for
Peter. God has indeed worked through us in this season.
We've traveled this road with Christ. It's not our
achievements or goals that are at stake. This isn't a
competition or a bucket list to complete. It's God's work of
reconciliation, which, even in small ways, has begun in us
anew, especially as we admit how we have fallen short.

Isaiah 49:1–6
Psalm 71:1–2,3–4a,5ab–6ab,15,17
John 13:21–33,36–38

Wednesday

APRIL 8

• WEDNESDAY OF HOLY WEEK •

For your sake I bear insult,
and shame covers my face.
I have become an outcast to my brothers,
a stranger to my mother's sons,
because zeal for your house consumes me,
and the insults of those who blaspheme you fall upon me.
—PSALM 69:8–10

It's not over. Throughout the world today, women, men, and children are suffering for the sake of Christ. Persecuted, insulted, confined, and threatened, they cling to him; they bear his wounds. Walking with Christ during Holy Week, I am walking with them, as well.

Isaiah 50:4–9a
Psalm 69:8–10,21–22,31,33–34
Matthew 26:14–25

Thursday

APRIL 9

Our blessing cup is a communion with the Blood of Christ.
—*See* 1 CORINTHIANS 10:16

As homeschoolers, we did our share of science experimentation. Electricity was a favorite. To see a lightbulb powered by nothing more than a lemon, a potato, or a solution of some sort is always exciting. We learned that this mysterious power isn't magic; it's there in things. When we tap into it—no more darkness. As I look around the congregation at Mass tonight, as I contemplate my brothers and sisters around the world, I am amazed and grateful that Jesus has made us one. It's his blood and sacrificial love binding us together and powering us to go out into a dark world. *Ite, missa est*—"We are sent."

CHRISM MASS:
Isaiah 61:1–3a,6a,8b–9
Psalm 89:21–22,25,27
Revelation 1:5–8
Luke 4:16–21

EVENING MASS OF THE
LORD'S SUPPER:
Exodus 12:1–8,11–14
Psalm 116:12–13,15–16bc,17–18
(see 1 Corinthians 10:16)
1 Corinthians 11:23–26
John 13:1–15

Friday

APRIL 10

So Pilate said to him, "Then you are a king?" Jesus answered, "You say I am a king. For this I was born and for this I came into the world, to testify to the truth. Everyone who belongs to the truth listens to my voice." Pilate said to him, "What is truth?"

—JOHN 18:37–38

There are so many mysteries about my faith, so many questions I can't answer. Even some that I thought I could answer yesterday may confound me today. God at once comforts and challenges me, and I wonder if I can ever grasp the truth at all. But through it all, one thing remains. The one thing I can't push away, ignore, or rationalize is the cross, and Jesus of Nazareth nailed to it. There it is: truth.

Isaiah 52:13—53:12
Psalm 31:2,6,12–13,15–16,17,25
Hebrews 4:14–16; 5:7–9
John 18:1—19:42

*If, then, we have died with Christ, we believe that we shall
also live with him.*
—ROMANS 6:8

I don't remember my baptism as a tiny baby, dying and rising
with Christ. This Holy Saturday liturgy gives me a chance to
remember with all of God's people. We remember being
rescued through waters; we remember God's power to bring
life to dry bones; we remember light, victorious through
darkness. We remember, and we see new
Christians—immersed and breaking free through those
waters, pointing the way to light and freedom for all of us.

VIGIL:
Genesis 1:1—2:2 or 1:1,26–31a
Psalm 104:1–2,5–6,10,12,13–14,24,35 or
33:4–5,6–7,12–13,20–22
Genesis 22:1–18 or
22:1–2,9a,10–13,15–18
Psalm 16:5,8,9–10,11
Exodus 14:15—15:1
Exodus 15:1–2,3–4,5–6,17–18 (1b)
Isaiah 54:5–14
Psalm 30:2,4,5–6,11–12,13 (2a)

Isaiah 55:1–11
Isaiah 12:2–3,4,5–6
Baruch 3:9–15,32—4:4
Psalm 19:8,9,10,11
Ezekiel 36:16–17a,18–28
Psalm 42:3,5; 43:3,4 or Isaiah
12:2–3,4bcd,5–6 or Psalm
51:12–13,14–15,18–19 (12a)
Romans 6:3–11
Psalm 118:1–2,16–17,22–23
Matthew 28:1–10

Sunday

APRIL 12

• EASTER SUNDAY OF THE RESURRECTION OF THE LORD •

So she ran and went to Simon Peter and to the other disciple whom Jesus loved, and told them, "They have taken the Lord from the tomb, and we don't know where they put him."

—JOHN 20:2

One of my favorite elements of the church's liturgical life at Easter is the Sequence. Perhaps you heard it chanted before the Gospel reading today: *Victimae paschali laudes.* The line—the question—that always stands out for me is this: *Dic nobis, Maria, quid vidisti in via?* "Tell us, Mary, what did you see on the way?" As we begin the journey of this Easter season, that's the question we are called to answer as well. We are filled with the life of the risen Lord not to keep it to ourselves but to witness to the world. Let's share the good news of what we've seen on the way.

Acts 10:34a,37–43
Psalm 118:1–2,16–17,22–23
Colossians 3:1–4 or 1 Corinthians 5:6b–8
John 20:1–9 or Matthew 28:1–10 or,
at an afternoon or evening Mass, Luke 24:13–35

God raised this Jesus; of this we are all witnesses.
—ACTS 2:32

Every time I decide that I have a pretty good memory, my
children prove me wrong. They'll relate some story from the
past, then say, "You remember that, right, Mom?" And I
hardly ever do. It's good that we don't carry the weight of our
histories alone. We need others to help fill in the gaps. I
witness to Christ not just as an individual but also as part of
the Body of Christ. All these witnesses help me remember
what I forget (or ignore); they illuminate what has receded
into the shadows. Of Jesus and his great love that breaks
through sin and death—we are all witnesses.

Acts 2:14,22–33
Psalm 16:1–2a and 5,7–8,9–10,11
Matthew 28:8–15

Tuesday

APRIL 14

Jesus said to her, "Woman, why are you weeping? Whom are you looking for?" She thought it was the gardener and said to him, "Sir, if you carried him away, tell me where you laid him, and I will take him." Jesus said to her, "Mary!"
—JOHN 20:15–16

When does Mary recognize Jesus? What does it take to bring her out of her grief and break through her expectations? When she hears him call her name.

Acts 2:36–41
Psalm 33:4–5,18–19,20,22
John 20:11–18

⇒ 136 ⇐

But Peter looked intently at him, as did John, and said, "Look at us." He paid attention to them, expecting to receive something from them. Peter said, "I have neither silver nor gold, but what I do have I give you: in the name of Jesus Christ the Nazorean, rise and walk."

—ACTS 3:4–6

Even as I downsize and purge, I'm aware that I still have too much stuff. Stuff that doesn't matter. For today I will have encounters with people. I might run into a few, or it might be a busy day full of people. What do I bring to those encounters? Nothing material is of importance as I meet another person on the journey, broken in some way (as we all are). What do I have to give? Only what is poured through me in the name of the risen Lord: the power of love.

Acts 3:1–10
Psalm 105:1–2,3–4,6–7,8–9
Luke 24:13–35

Thursday

APRIL 16

• THURSDAY WITHIN THE OCTAVE OF EASTER •

"Why are you troubled? And why do questions arise in your hearts?
Look at my hands and my feet, that it is I myself."
—LUKE 24:38–39

The garage doors had been inoperable for months, mostly
because I thought it would be a costly repair. A handyman
came, snapped a part into place, pushed a button, and it was
done. I was elated at the simplicity and zero cost, but a little
embarrassed that I'd not figured it out myself. In a similar
way, I think about the distance between my own weakness
and God's promises. It seems like a pretty big space and can
be troubling. But during the Easter season, I'm reminded that
bridging the gap might not be as fraught as I'm tempted to
imagine. I hear Jesus' words, and yes, I'm a little abashed
about my resistance. But more than anything else, I'm joyful.
And relieved.

Acts 3:11–26
Psalm 8:2ab and 5,6–7,8–9
Luke 24:35–48

Friday

APRIL 17

• FRIDAY WITHIN THE OCTAVE OF EASTER •

Jesus said to them, "Come, have breakfast."
—JOHN 21:12

Such difficulties and struggles lie in the past. The suffering
we've seen, the darkness, the confusion, the dashed hopes.
But look! Who is there on the beach next to a simple burning
fire, waiting, welcoming, and yes, alive?

Acts 4:1–12
Psalm 118:1–2,4,22–24,25–27a
John 21:1–14

When they heard that he was alive and had been seen by her,
they did not believe.
—MARK 16:11

It was just a couple of weeks before Ash Wednesday when my husband died. That year, Lent was easy. But then Easter came around, and I was challenged. Still walking around in a fog of sadness—my own and, more important, my children's—I heard the Good News. Surrounded by white, gold, lilies, and joyful music, I couldn't respond in an unambiguous, unconflicted way. For the first time in my life, I had to really think about what I was asked to say, think about the response to this news that I'd offered so reflexively and unthinkingly in the past. Did I really believe it? Could I sing *Alleluia* and mean it?

Acts 4:13–21
Psalm 118:1,14–15ab,16–18,19–21
Mark 16:9–15

Sunday

APRIL 19

• SECOND SUNDAY OF EASTER (OR SUNDAY OF DIVINE MERCY) •

Blessed be the God and Father of our Lord Jesus Christ, who in his great mercy gave us a new birth to a living hope through the resurrection of Jesus Christ from the dead.
—1 PETER 1:3

If you have ever worshipped in an Eastern Catholic or Orthodox liturgy, you might walk away with the word *mercy* ringing in your ears. The service repeats "Have mercy upon us. . . . Lord, have mercy" more times than you can count . . . maybe too many times? Do I need *that* much mercy? Well, speaking for myself, yes, I really do. How many times during the day do I say no to grace? That's what I'm begging to have mercy for—all those noes that have kept me in place or even taken me further away. But with the risen, living Lord, there's always mercy, and never too much, ever.

Acts 2:42–47
Psalm 118:2–4,13–15,22–24
1 Peter 1:3–9
John 20:19–31

Monday

APRIL 20

There was a Pharisee named Nicodemus, a ruler of the Jews. He came to Jesus at night and said to him, "Rabbi, we know that you are a teacher who has come from God, for no one can do these signs that you are doing unless God is with him."
—JOHN 3:1–2

Nicodemus belonged to a group whose members were, at the least, skeptical of Jesus, and, at the most, growing in opposition. But Nicodemus was still intrigued, still moved, still curious, still drawn. So in the middle of the night he followed the nudges and urgings of his heart and sought Jesus. During the course of a day, each of us senses similar promptings of the Spirit: to explore a spiritual question, to turn to Jesus in prayer, to reach out in charity. How do we respond?

Acts 4:23–31
Psalm 2:1–3,4–7a,7b–9
John 3:1–8

Tuesday

APRIL 21

• ST. ANSELM, BISHOP AND DOCTOR OF THE CHURCH •

The community of believers was of one heart and mind, and no one claimed that any of his possessions was his own, but they had everything in common.

—ACTS 4:32

I consider what I own—not simply material things but my abilities, my thoughts, and the life of my spirit. What am I hoarding? Opening myself to the generous life of the risen Christ, I ponder how I can let that life flow through me, binding me more closely to those in need.

Acts 4:32–37
Psalm 93:1ab,1cd–2,5
John 3:7b–15

Wednesday

APRIL 22

Taste and see how good the LORD is;
blessed the man who takes refuge in him.
—PSALM 34:9

I was sitting in a church one weekday. Another woman came and sat down in a pew across the church. She looked around at the images of the saints, at the crucifix, at the other people praying. She seemed curious, relaxed, interested. Not intense. She picked up a missalette and flipped through it quickly. Then she did so again, this time more slowly, pausing at times. Finally, she went to the beginning and read slowly. Who knows what brought her into the church that day. Who knows what seeds were planted and what she took away as, perhaps, without fully knowing what she was seeking, she took refuge.

Acts 5:17–26
Psalm 34:2–3,4–5,6–7,8–9
John 3:16–21

Thursday

APRIL 23

*But Peter and the Apostles said in reply, "We must obey God
rather than men."*
—ACTS 5:29

St. Marie de l'Incarnation was one of the great figures of the
French missions to Canada in the seventeenth century. She
was an Ursuline sister, but before that she had been married
and widowed and had a son who eventually entered religious
life himself. In one of her many letters published in *From
Mother to Son*, she encouraged her son with a phrase that, it
seems to me, succinctly characterizes the apostolic life from
Acts to the present. She tells him that she prays his actions
are Spirit led, unbound by human concerns, and guided by "a
holy audacity accompanied by divine prudence." What a
powerful way of framing our own discernment, even today.

Acts 5:27–33
Psalm 34:2,9,17–18,19–20
John 3:31–36

And all day long, both at the temple and in their homes, they did not stop teaching and proclaiming the Christ, Jesus.
—ACTS 5:42

As a parent, teacher, and teaching parent, I'm all about the teachable moment, probably to a tedious, predictable extent: "Look, a leaf. Let's talk about the biology of the leaf, the etymology of the word *leaf*, and the history of leaves in literature." Yes, just call me the Fun Mom. The witness of the apostles reminds me how much there is to teach through our lives: teachable moments in which, through my actions, my treatment of others, and maybe even my words, I have an opportunity to proclaim the love and mercy of Jesus.

Acts 5:34–42
Psalm 27:1,4,13–14
John 6:1–15

Saturday

APRIL 25

• ST. MARK, EVANGELIST •

So humble yourselves under the mighty hand of God, that he may exalt
you in due time.
—1 PETER 5:6

The call of worldly success and acceptance runs strong and
deep, even within the context of Christian communities. It's
hard to resist. The only way to resist it is to keep our eyes on
the cross and remember the way of humility we follow. John
Henry Newman, in his *Meditations on Christian Doctrine*, puts it
all in perspective for us: "Therefore, I will trust Him.
Whatever, wherever I am, I can never be thrown away. If I am
in sickness, my sickness may serve Him; in perplexity, my
perplexity may serve Him; if I am in sorrow, my sorrow may
serve Him. He does nothing in vain. . . . He knows what He
is about."

1 Peter 5:5b–14
Psalm 89:2–3,6–7,16–17
Mark 16:15–20

Sunday

APRIL 26

• THIRD SUNDAY OF EASTER •

Beloved: if you invoke as Father him who judges impartially according to each one's works, conduct yourselves with reverence during the time of your sojourning.
—1 PETER 1:17

Perspective really is everything. Realizing that my perspective from my viewpoint in this specific time and place is limited and narrow is essential, not only to my mental health but also to my spiritual life. Here, Peter uses one word that reminds me of that in a powerful way: "sojourning." This place and time? They're not forever. My home is elsewhere. In times of suffering, or even in times of joy, that's exactly the perspective I need.

Acts 2:14,22–33
Psalm 16:1–2,5,7–8,9–10,11 (11a)
1 Peter 1:17–21
Luke 24:13–35

Remove from me the way of falsehood,
and favor me with your law.
—PSALM 119:29

We can't trust ourselves, but then again, we can and we must.
Growing as human beings, growing in faith, involves a
constant dynamic of discovering what is authentic and good
in ourselves and weeding out the false and destructive. This
psalm is a prayer we might offer gingerly, not really sure if
we want it answered. Do we actually want to leave the
falsehood and inauthenticity behind?

Acts 6:8–15
Psalm 119:23–24,26–27,29–30
John 6:22–29

• ST. PETER CHANEL, PRIEST AND MARTYR * ST. LOUIS GRIGNION
DE MONTFORT, PRIEST •

*For the bread of God is that which comes down from heaven and gives
life to the world.*
—JOHN 6:33

I've seen videos of hummingbird feeders surrounded by a
crowd of happy, compatible, tiny birds. But not at my house.
My hummingbirds are incredibly territorial. One hovers in a
nearby tree waiting for another to approach, then
dive-bombs and drives the intruder away. Then it's back to
his post, without even taking a sip of nectar. I know they
feed, but I really don't know when. All I see is the battle, with
everyone left hungry, it seems. Jesus offers himself as the
Bread of Life, with more than enough love and grace for each
and every one of us. What anger, what resentment, what
envy, what urge for isolation is keeping us from being
nourished by the abundance he offers?

Acts 7:51—8:1a
Psalm 31:3cd–4,6,7b and 8a,17,21ab
John 6:30–35

Jesus said to the crowds, "I am the bread of life; whoever comes to me will never hunger, and whoever believes in me will never thirst."

—JOHN 6:35

St. Catherine of Siena's visions and writings incorporate rich, sometimes even startling, imagery. Take blood. We are accustomed to thinking about being saved or even washed clean by the blood of Christ, but Catherine takes it a step beyond. Describing the life of a disciple in *The Dialogue*, she writes, "Indeed, they go into battle filled and inebriated with the blood of Christ crucified." Startling, yes; but think about it. Drunkenness implies a lack of control, of being taken over. While we normally (and rightfully) see that in a negative light, when it comes to faith—when it comes to Jesus—it's what he offers: to fill me, to satiate me, to be my very life.

Acts 8:1b–8
Psalm 66:1–3a,4–5,6–7a
John 6:35–40

"I am the living bread that came down from heaven, says the Lord;
whoever eats this bread will live forever; and the bread that I will give is
my Flesh for the life of the world."
—JOHN 6:51

There are so many prayers to offer after receiving the Lord in
communion. So much gratitude and awe at the One who has
come to me. So many needs and so much hunger we ask him
to satisfy. So many people to lift up in prayer. So many
things, in fact, that I often find myself speechless, with only
the simplest of prayers but one that covers just about
everything: *Jesus, Peace.*

Acts 8:26–40
Psalm 66:8–9,16–17,20
John 6:44–51

Friday

MAY 1

• ST. JOSEPH THE WORKER •

*Jesus said to them, "Amen, amen, I say to you, unless you eat the Flesh
of the Son of Man and drink his Blood, you do not have life within you.
Whoever eats my Flesh and drinks my Blood has eternal life, and I will
raise him on the last day."*
—JOHN 6:53–54

Receiving the Lord in the Eucharist thousands of times since
I was a child, do I take it—and him—for granted? I have to
admit, yes, at times. I pray for the grace to be startled out of
complacency the next time the gift is offered, for openness to
the power flowing from the Bread of Life.

Acts 9:1–20 or Genesis 1:26—2:3 or
Colossians 3:14–15,17,23–24
Psalm 117:1bc,2
John 6:52–59 or Matthew 13:54–58

• ST. ATHANASIUS, BISHOP AND DOCTOR OF THE CHURCH •

The Church throughout all Judea, Galilee, and Samaria was at peace.
She was being built up and walked in the fear of the Lord, and with the
consolation of the Holy Spirit she grew in numbers.
—ACTS 9:31

A parish near me has an interesting set of stained-glass
windows. In the center is the scene of Pentecost. The power
of the Holy Spirit, pictured as beams of light from a dove,
flows down into the Pentecost scene and from there to two
side windows. One of the side windows depicts St. Paul—the
patron of this diocese—at work, and the other, St. Francis
Xavier—the patron of this particular parish—in the missions.
It is a lovely depiction of the continuity of the growing
church and missionary discipleship—from the Holy Spirit to
the apostles to us, wherever we are.

Acts 9:31–42
Psalm 116:12–13,14–15,16–17
John 6:60–69

Sunday

MAY 3

• FOURTH SUNDAY OF EASTER •

When he was insulted, he returned no insult; when he suffered, he did not
threaten; instead, he handed himself over to the one who judges justly.
—1 PETER 2:23

I was present at Mass at a local convent, during which a sister
was making her final profession of vows. Vowed religious
life, the bishop said, is also a radical sign of grace and mercy.
He said that the heart of a religious is bound in love to "the
poor Christ, the chaste Christ, the obedient Christ" and is to
be a sign of that to a world that is often uncomprehending
and even hostile. I'm not a vowed religious, but I am a
disciple of Jesus. In whatever way my particular state of life
makes possible, I'm called to this as well: to imitate the poor,
chaste, and obedient Christ, patient and humble, resisting
evil with good.

Acts 2:14a,36–41
Psalm 23:1–3a, 3b–4,5,6
1 Peter 2:20b–25
John 10:1–10

⇒ 155 ⇐

Monday

MAY 4

Then will I go in to the altar of God,
the God of my gladness and joy;
Then will I give you thanks upon the harp.
—PSALM 43:4

We're right in the thick of sacrament season, and perhaps it's reviving memories of your own sacramental celebrations. Here are mine: I almost drowned after my first communion (or I felt like it, struggling in the pool of the family hosting a post-Mass reception), and I got violently ill after my confirmation (probably from a bad meatball). Not a lot of gladness and joy there, on the surface. But it's fitting in a way. We can idealize these moments—and truly, they are wonderful—but as life moves on, we understand that the gladness and joy of encountering the Lord and engaging with his grace happen in less than ideal circumstances, in the tough, imperfect reality of life.

Acts 11:1–18
Psalm 42:2–3; 43:3–4
John 10:11–18

*"How long are you going to keep us in suspense? If you are the Christ,
tell us plainly." Jesus answered them, "I told you and you do not believe.
The works I do in my Father's name testify to me."*
—JOHN 10:24–25

To live as though the suspense is over, as if I really have
heard and, more important, listened to Jesus tell me who he
is—can I do that today? Can I set aside fear and engage with
what comes my way with boldness and confidence, joyfully
trusting in Jesus' saving, healing presence?

Acts 11:19–26
Psalm 87:1b–3,4–5,6–7
John 10:22–30

May the peoples praise you, O God;
may all the peoples praise you!
—PSALM 67:6

This psalm is a good example of why it's better for me not to
be left to my own prayer devices, praying only for myself,
my kids, and other people I happen to know about. These are
all good things! But as I enter into this psalm of praise (and
all the psalms), my prayer is grounded and directed to a
bigger picture, of which I am a tiny part. What will I do
today, and why will I do it? Perhaps today my vision will
expand and reach beyond my own walls. Perhaps today I can
pray and praise not simply with my own joy but together
with all believers—our joy, our song, our home.

Acts 12:24—13:5a
Psalm 67:2–3,5,6,8
John 12:44–50

*So Paul got up, motioned with his hand, and said, "Fellow children of
Israel and you others who are God-fearing, listen."*
—ACTS 13:16

Every time, at every step of the way, Paul begins to tell the
story of Jesus on familiar ground in familiar ways. He goes to
the synagogues and reminds his listeners of their history and
the hopes they have, based on that history. Only then does
he share the good news of how God has, indeed, fulfilled
those hopes and answered their centuries-old prayers. So it is
that the good news of salvation comes to me. God knows
me; God reveals himself to me in my life right now. Listening
patiently from this place, I can hear—and understand.

Acts 13:13–25
Psalm 89:2–3,21–22,25,27
John 13:16–20

*In my Father's house there are many dwelling places. If there were not,
would I have told you that I am going to prepare a place for you?*
—JOHN 14:1–2

I am not a "house person," but I do like houses. By that I
mean that I have neither renovating nor decorating skills, but
I do have that constant, subconscious desire to search for
"the one." We've been in our present place for a few years and
when I bought it, I proclaimed, "This is it. No more!" But
who am I kidding? I still looked. Just to see what was out
there, right? Then one day, I was moved—by grace—to
choose to stop looking, stop feeding dissatisfaction with this
earthly home. Maybe now I'll find more space to focus on
another, lasting dwelling place.

Acts 13:26–33
Psalm 2:6–7,8–9,10–11ab
John 14:1–6

Saturday

MAY 9

So they shook the dust from their feet in protest against them and went to Iconium. The disciples were filled with joy and the Holy Spirit.
—ACTS 13:51–52

When to persist in a situation, and when to walk away? This narrative about Paul and Barnabas doesn't give us a step-by-step process or formula, but it does offer a general vision in two respects. First, conforming to God's will in a given situation just might mean walking away. Second, surprising joy. Even when we are rejected, if this is the Lord's will and we are faithful to Christ, there can be joy.

Acts 13:44–52
Psalm 98:1,2–3ab,3cd–4
John 14:7–14

Sunday

MAY 10

• FIFTH SUNDAY OF EASTER •

Come to him, a living stone, rejected by human beings but chosen and precious in the sight of God, and, like living stones, let yourselves be built into a spiritual house to be a holy priesthood to offer spiritual sacrifices acceptable to God through Jesus Christ.

—1 PETER 2:4–5

Our culture's emphasis on the power and potential of individual effort has influenced how we think about spirituality, hasn't it? Make a plan. Take control over your life. Just do it! But what does Peter say? "Let yourselves be built. . . ." Let God do it. We have a role to play, of course. But faith and spiritual growth are ultimately gifts. Through prayer, connecting with Christ through the sacraments, meeting him in those in need, we open ourselves to his power, place ourselves in his hands, and allow him to build us up.

Acts 6:1–7
Psalm 33:1–2,4–5,18–19
1 Peter 2:4–9
John 14:1–12

*Whoever loves me will keep my word, and my Father will love him, and
we will come to him and make our dwelling with him.*
—JOHN 14:23

I love traveling, and I love researching travel. When I'm
headed to a new destination, I've done so much research that
I think I know what I'll be encountering. But, of course, I
don't. What I encounter will be vaguely familiar from all my
reading but so much more. I'll come back with a new set of
experiences and real understanding and hopefully be
changed in a good way. The most accurate ideas fade once
you've experienced reality. It's the same with faith. Knowing
about Jesus is good, but it's not the same as knowing him,
dwelling in him, and living the life to which he invites me.

Acts 14:5–18
Psalm 115:1–2,3–4,15–16
John 14:21–26

Tuesday

MAY 12

• ST. NEREUS AND ST. ACHILLEUS, MARTYRS • ST. PANCRAS, MARTYR •

Let all your works give you thanks, O LORD,
and let your faithful ones bless you.
—PSALM 145:10

The time I broke my finger was inconvenient and aggravating, mostly because the incident was absolutely stupid and preventable. In subsequent weeks, I retraced my steps many times, wishing I'd just done that one little thing differently. However, I discovered something interesting, albeit reluctantly: Instead of simply regretting and wishing life were other than it is, I try to be present in these new places my action has taken me—this doctor's office, this pharmacy, that "place" of discomfort and inconvenience. In those places where I am, not wishing to be elsewhere, I let God teach me and find ways to offer thanks. Because here is where I am, stupid broken finger and all.

Acts 14:19–28
Psalm 145:10–11,12–13ab,21
John 14:27–31a

164

Wednesday

MAY 13

• OUR LADY OF FATIMA •

I am the vine, you are the branches. Whoever remains in me and I in him will bear much fruit.
—JOHN 15:5

My son loves woodpeckers and always pauses during a hike to search the trees when he hears one tapping away at work. He wondered, though, how their little heads don't just explode from all the force. So we looked it up and discovered that it's just the way they are made. They were created and designed to live and flourish in a certain way. And so are we. We can look at great acts of love and sacrifice and wonder, *How is it possible for a person to give that much?* Jesus reminds us that we are created to be connected to him, designed to receive his love and share it—not only surviving the experience but thriving, growing, and reaching ever upward.

Acts 15:1–6
Psalm 122:1–2,3–4ab,4cd–5
John 15:1–8

Thursday

MAY 14

• ST. MATTHIAS, APOSTLE •

This I command you: love one another.
—JOHN 15:17

What is it we say when we want to express deadly dullness?
"It's like watching paint dry." Well, the other day, I did watch
some paint dry, and actually, it was not the most boring thing
I've ever done. That second coat initially looked to be a
completely different shade than the original, but as the
minutes passed, the colors melded and the texture smoothed
out. It was a slow and almost imperceptible process, but
change did happen. Jesus has commanded me to love. But
does it really change anything? Here in daily life, the impact
of obeying that commandment can be hard to discern. But
when I am patient, I can sense that life becomes something
different when forgiveness and mercy reign. Slow in coming,
perhaps, but still inarguably different than what was
there before.

Acts 1:15–17,20–26
Psalm 113:1–2,3–4,5–6,7–8
John 15:9–17

Friday

MAY 15

• ST. ISIDORE •

I will give you thanks among the peoples, O LORD,
I will chant your praise among the nations.
For your mercy towers to the heavens,
and your faithfulness to the skies.
—PSALM 57:10–11

What a mystery. Amidst the suffering, the questions, and the
mistakes, here I am, living one more day of life in God's
creation. In this moment, I can set aside irritations and
worries. In this moment, I can let God in, accept his mercy
and begin again, grateful.

Acts 15:22–31
Psalm 57:8–9,10,12
John 15:12–17

When they came to Mysia, they tried to go on into Bithynia, but the Spirit of Jesus did not allow them, so they crossed through Mysia and came down to Troas.

—ACTS 16:7–8

How did they know? What did they experience that indicated that the Spirit was at work, preventing this, allowing that, and guiding in this way? We're not told. Perhaps Paul and Barnabas might have found it difficult to explain themselves. For me, discerning involves a combination of what I know is right and true from God's Word and the Spirit's guidance through the church, framed at all times by love for others and trust in God. The fact is, he is in control, and I am not.

Acts 16:1–10
Psalm 100:1b–2,3,5
John 15:18–21

⇒ 168 ⇐

Sunday

MAY 17

• SIXTH SUNDAY OF EASTER •

Always be ready to give an explanation to anyone who asks you for a reason for your hope, but do it with gentleness and reverence.
—1 PETER 3:15–16

When we think of defending our faith, we often think of it in terms of explaining propositions and ideas. But perhaps the more frequent call to defend our faith comes in the ebb and flow of ordinary life. In times of stress and trouble, how is it that we're staying calm? When we're hurt, how in the world are we able to forgive? Surrounded by strangers, we welcome them with a smile. How do we do it? What's the source of our peace? Are we ready to share that Good News—the reason for our hope?

Acts 8:5–8,14–17
Psalm 66:1–3,4–5,6–7,16,20
1 Peter 3:15–18
John 14:15–21

Monday

MAY 18

• ST. JOHN I, POPE AND MARTYR •

I have told you this so that when their hour comes you may
remember that I told you.
—JOHN 16:4a

The basic task I face each day is to discern God's will. How would the Lord have me respond to each situation I face? How do I do that? Upon what do I base my discernment? There are, to be sure, countless voices and forces to which I could listen and turn for guidance. But if I really want to be my best self—which is the self that God created—it's to Jesus I must turn first, last, and always, remembering what he has told me.

Acts 16:11–15
Psalm 149:1b–2,3–4,5–6a,9b
John 15:26—16:4a

He took them in at that hour of the night and bathed their wounds; then he and all his family were baptized at once. He brought them up into his house and provided a meal and with his household rejoiced at having come to faith in God.
—ACTS 16:33–34

On a certain day, a jailer left his home in Philippi and went to work, probably expecting a day like any other. What reason would he have to expect anything different? But by the end of the day, his life had been turned upside down by an earthquake, broken chains, and the power of God. What doors might God open, what chains might he shatter in my life today, in ways that I could never, ever expect?

Acts 16:22–34
Psalm 138:1–2ab,2cde–3,7c–8
John 16:5–11

Wednesday
MAY 20

• ST. BERNARDINE OF SIENA, PRIEST •

What therefore you unknowingly worship, I proclaim to you.
—ACTS 17:23

I recently watched an episode of a television show set far in the future, amid spaceships and droids, in which a character was wearing, of all things, a St. Christopher medal. We live in a self-proclaimed secular culture, but when confronted with death, people still say things such as, "Oh, I just feel she's watching over me." Flannery O'Connor writes in a letter in *The Habit of Being*, "I have noticed that the girls at the local college adore to have ceremonies in which they light candles or hold lighted candles. Any excuse will do." God created us; God calls us. The risen Lord dwells among his people whether they recognize him or not. The pull is there, the pull is strong, and we're all responding in one way or another.

Acts 17:15,22—18:1
Psalm 148:1–2,11–12,13,14
John 16:12–15

Thursday

MAY 21

• THE ASCENSION OF THE LORD •

"Men of Galilee, why are you standing there looking at the sky?"
—ACTS 1:11

This has got to be one of my favorite moments from the entire Bible. It's a simple, direct question that I probably need to post in a visible place so I see it every single day, several times a day. Hey, you! Why are you standing around wondering what to do? Jesus is risen; Jesus has given you a mission; Jesus may seem as if he is gone, but he isn't. He's dwelling here with you right now, empowering you to love, give, and serve. Get moving!

THE ASCENSION OF THE LORD:
Acts 1:1–11
Psalm 47:2–3,6–7,8–9
Ephesians 1:17–23
Matthew 28:16–20

EASTER WEEKDAY:
Acts 18:1–8
Psalm 98:1,2–3ab,3cd–4
John 16:16–20

Friday

MAY 22

• ST. RITA OF CASCIA, RELIGIOUS •

*So you also are now in anguish. But I will see you again, and your
hearts will rejoice, and no one will take your joy away from you.*
—JOHN 16:22

I have had my share of intense spiritual experiences, of
encounters with the Lord that changed me and assured me of
the reality of God's love and promise. But then what
happens? I change. Daily life courses on with its demands.
The joy is gone. Everyone needs something different to stay
anchored in the Lord's peace and to hold on to those
moments of the Lord's touch. I need material reminders such
as crosses on the wall, holy cards strewn on my desk, and
candles. Most of all I need time—a moment here and a
minute there—to quiet myself, recollect, and simply say his
name—*Jesus.*

Acts 18:9–18
Psalm 47:2–3,4–5,6–7
John 16:20–23

Saturday

MAY 23

All you peoples, clap your hands;
shout to God with cries of gladness.
—PSALM 47:2

There are so many reasons to praise God today. So much to
be grateful for, so much beauty. Today I will join with the
psalmist and all those through the centuries who have
echoed these words. I'll begin my day with those cries of
gladness for the Lord and all he's done.

Acts 18:23–28
Psalm 47:2–3,8–9,10
John 16:23b–28

Sunday

MAY 24

• THE ASCENSION OF THE LORD • SEVENTH SUNDAY OF EASTER •

All these devoted themselves with one accord to prayer, together with some
women, and Mary the mother of Jesus, and his brothers.
—ACTS 1:14

And so begins the first novena. Some might treat a novena in
a superstitious way, like a good-luck chain that cannot be
broken without dire consequences. But, of course, that's not
the power of a novena, our nine-day prayer in imitation of
the apostles and the Blessed Virgin. They had just
experienced an astounding reality: Jesus crucified, then risen,
now ascended, and clearly intending for them to continue his
mission on earth. But how? What to do? How to proceed
from there? When in doubt: pray.

SEVENTH SUNDAY OF EASTER:
Acts 1:12–14
Psalm 27:1,4,7–8
1 Peter 4:13–16
John 17:1–11a

THE ASCENSION OF THE LORD:
Acts 1:1–11
Psalm 47:2–3,6–7,8–9
Ephesians 1:17–23
Matthew 28:16–20

Monday

MAY 25

• ST. BEDE THE VENERABLE, PRIEST AND DOCTOR OF THE CHURCH •
ST. GREGORY VII, POPE • ST. MARY MAGDALENE DE' PAZZI, VIRGIN •

*In the world you will have trouble, but take courage, I have
conquered the world.*
—JOHN 16:33

Over the past several years, my two youngest sons have
moved between homeschooling and brick-and-mortar
schools a couple of times for various good reasons. But the
initial decision to leave school and try something different
came at the end of a protracted process of discernment.
What eventually made all the difference was confronting my
incorrect assumption that we were looking to land in a
perfect, aggravation-free place. But there's no such place, is
there? The question is, rather, which aggravation will we
pick? If our focus is avoiding trouble and suffering, is that
going to help us be formed in the way of Jesus?

Acts 19:1–8
Psalm 68:2–3ab,4–5acd,6–7ab
John 16:29–33

Tuesday

MAY 26

• ST. PHILIP NERI, PRIEST •

But now, compelled by the Spirit, I am going to Jerusalem. What will
happen to me there I do not know.
—ACTS 20:22

The process of creating works of art—painting, music,
film—is fascinating. It's also scary, from a creative
perspective, to see how much serendipity and what looks like
chance—whether it be the quirks of a patron, scarce supplies,
or the limited schedule of an actor—work (or fall) together
to produce something great. Planning and preparation are
important, but the end result of what I'm up to—whether it
be a piece of writing, cooking dinner, raising my children, or
simply the course of an ordinary day—is not under my
control. What will happen to me today? I don't know the
specifics, I can't plan it, but I know I want it to align with
God's will and goodness. So here I go, open to the Spirit.

Acts 20:17–27
Psalm 68:10–11,20–21
John 17:1–11a

Wednesday

MAY 27

• ST. AUGUSTINE OF CANTERBURY, BISHOP •

As you sent me into the world, so I sent them into the world.
—JOHN 17:18

The world is a big place and an enormous mission field. But, indeed, the world is where Jesus sends us. Missionary saints such as St. Augustine of Canterbury, a Benedictine monk who took the gospel to sixth-century England, lived out this calling. But here's where it starts: with my own neighbors, the people I will encounter today in ordinary ways and places. That's where "the world" starts. That's the first place Jesus sends me: out my door and down my own street.

Acts 20:28–38
Psalm 68:29–30,33–35a,35bc–36ab
John 17:11b–19

Thursday

MAY 28

And I have given them the glory you gave me, so that they may be one, as we are one, I in them and you in me, that they may be brought to perfection as one, that the world may know that you sent me, and that you loved them even as you loved me.

—JOHN 17:22–23

There they were, in a Tokyo food shop: the infamous hundred-dollar-a-piece cantaloupes. What was that about? What a weird culture! Well, then I learned that these cantaloupes are given as gifts: a housewarming gift, after a great professional accomplishment, after a return from a long journey. They're of perfect shape, with no blemishes—so that perfection symbolizes great hope and joy. Maybe not so weird after all—just different. May my choices today be a similar gift, one that I share with the world, reflecting as much as possible, the perfect love of Jesus Christ.

Acts 22:30; 23:6–11
Psalm 16:1–2a,5,7–8,9–10,11
John 17:20–26

Friday

MAY 29

He said to him the third time, "Simon, son of John, do you love me?"
Peter was distressed that he had said to him a third time, "Do you love
me?" and he said to him, "Lord, you know everything; you know that I
love you." Jesus said to him, "Feed my sheep."
—JOHN 21:17

In the midst of our Easter joy and our openness to sharing
the Good News, something might still hold us back. It's a
fact: we are sinners; we're unworthy. Who would listen to us?
Right in the midst of our unworthiness, Jesus meets us just as
he met Peter. Peter had denied Jesus three times, so three
times Jesus addressed him, inviting him to greater
confidence. Then Jesus sent him out, leaving the past behind.

Acts 25:13b–21
Psalm 103:1–2,11–12,19–20ab
John 21:15–19

≥ 181 ≤

Saturday

MAY 30

[Paul] remained for two full years in his lodgings. He received all who came to him, and with complete assurance and without hindrance he proclaimed the Kingdom of God and taught about the Lord Jesus Christ.
—ACTS 28:30–31

Paul didn't let being under house arrest get in his way of proclaiming the kingdom. No matter what the circumstances, no matter how restricted and confined and limited the moment may seem, Jesus is always present. Empowered by the Spirit, we can *always* share the love of Jesus, in whatever moment, in whatever odd, unlikely, or even undesirable place we may find ourselves.

Acts 28:16–20,30–31
Psalm 11:4,5,7
John 21:20–25

Sunday

MAY 31

• PENTECOST SUNDAY •

When the time for Pentecost was fulfilled, they were all
in one place together.
—ACTS 2:1

There is much we could focus on in this Pentecost narrative:
the wind, the tongues of fire, the miracle of understanding.
Yet what gets my attention every time is the issue of fear.
Why were the apostles in one place together? Because they
were afraid, so afraid in fact that they locked themselves up
in that place. But then, filled with the Holy Spirit, they
threw themselves into the middle of another previously
frightening place—the place of crucifixion—but now
empowered by love that knows no fear.

VIGIL:
Genesis 11:1–9 or Exodus 19:3–8a,16–20b
or Ezekiel 37:1–14 or Joel 3:1–5
Psalm 104:1–2,24,35,27–28,29,30
Romans 8:22–27
John 7:37–39

EXTENDED VIGIL:
Genesis 11:1–9
Psalm 33:10–11,12–13,14–15
Exodus 19:3–8a, 16–20b
Daniel 3:52,53,54,55 or Psalm 19:8,9,10,11

Ezekiel 37:1–14
Psalm 107:2–3,4–5,6–7,8–9
Joel 3:1–5
Psalm 104:1–2,24,35,27–28,29,30
Romans 8:22–27
John 7:37–39

DAY:
Acts 2:1–11
Psalm 104:1,24,29–30,31,34
1 Corinthians 12:3b–7,12–13
John 20:19–23

Monday

JUNE 1

• THE BLESSED VIRGIN MARY, MOTHER OF THE CHURCH
(NINTH WEEK IN ORDINARY TIME) •

*Standing by the cross of Jesus were his mother and his mother's sister,
Mary the wife of Clopas, and Mary of Magdala. When Jesus saw his
mother and the disciple there whom he loved, he said to his mother,
"Woman, behold, your son." Then he said to the disciple,
"Behold, your mother."*
—JOHN 19:25–27

The day after Pentecost, right before we step into Ordinary
Time, we're reminded that we are not alone. We've witnessed
victory over sin and death. We've embraced the mission;
we're ready to move forward into the world that is hungry for
what the Lord would share through us. What does it look
like to respond to Jesus, to be shaped as a disciple day in and
day out? Mary is here, teaching us what it looks like to
say yes.

Genesis 3:9–15,20 or Acts 1:12–14
Psalm 87:1–2,3,5,6–7
John 19:25–34

Tuesday

JUNE 2

• ST. MARCELLINUS AND ST. PETER, MARTYRS •

*But grow in grace and in the knowledge of our Lord and savior
Jesus Christ.*
—2 PETER 3:18

I was confident that teaching one of my kids to drive a manual transmission wouldn't be difficult. I didn't find driving a stick difficult, so how hard could it be to teach it? But we soon discovered that it was one thing to instinctively drive the thing and a completely different matter to communicate how to do it. Ultimately, my son had to learn the only way possible—living through jolts, surges forward, and mistakes. Words, listening to them and learning from them, can get us only so far. But to internalize the Word, grow in grace, and live in Jesus' way? We just have to commit to it and live it out day to day, grinding our gears along the way.

2 Peter 3:12–15a,17–18
Psalm 90:2,3–4,10,14,16
Mark 12:13–17

Wednesday
JUNE 3

• ST. CHARLES LWANGA AND COMPANIONS, MARTYRS •

[B]ear your share of hardship for the Gospel.
—2 TIMOTHY 1:8

For a time my youngest son participated in weekly boxing
training sessions. There was no actual contact, just an hour of
workouts with gloves and weights and whatever else they
use. It was hard. Afterward, he'd report on that week's
impossible challenges, exhausted. But as he talked, he was
still grinning, with not even a hint of wanting to quit.
Something about the coach's manner and presentation
evidently convinced a bunch of kids—for whom taking out
the trash is a major sacrifice—that their suffering had value.
Out of context, the suffering and hardship that love demands
might seem to be too much. But keeping Jesus front and
center, I can bear it, even if I don't always smile
about it. Maybe.

2 Timothy 1:1–3,6–12
Psalm 123:1b–2ab,2cdef
Mark 12:18–27

And when Jesus saw that [he] answered with understanding, he said to him, "You are not far from the Kingdom of God." And no one dared to ask him any more questions.
—MARK 12:34

We like to focus on the welcoming warmth of Jesus as we meet him in the Gospels, but there's definitely another side, and it comes out very clearly in Mark. The apostles and others are constantly mystified by Jesus' words and actions, and even a little afraid. It's why, I suppose, the "fear of the Lord" is a gift of the Holy Spirit: it's a sign that we recognize—even if we don't understand—the deep mystery of God's power and presence right here in our midst.

2 Timothy 2:8–15
Psalm 25:4–5ab,8–9,10,14
Mark 12:28–34

Friday

JUNE 5

*All Scripture is inspired by God and is useful for teaching, for refutation,
for correction, and for training in righteousness.*
—2 TIMOTHY 3:16

We were in a Baroque church in Mexico City that was
bursting with swirls of gold, vivid statuary, and cherubim
heads. But there was a particular feature of this one that
caught my eye. There were four large medallions in the
sanctuary, each depicting one of the evangelists with his
winged symbol: Matthew with an angel, Luke an ox, John an
eagle, and Mark a lion. Nothing unusual there. But what
made these stand out was that each of the human Gospel
writers was depicted seated on top of these winged symbols.
It was as if God's Word was flying high and racing right
toward me, full of energy and power—a little dangerous.
Was I ready?

2 Timothy 3:10–17
Psalm 119:157,160,161,165,166,168
Mark 12:35–37

Saturday

JUNE 6

• ST. NORBERT, BISHOP •

A poor widow also came and put in two small coins worth a few cents.
—MARK 12:42

My friend on our summer Maine vacations had several older brothers, one of whom I thought was named "Nobbit." Years later I ran across today's saint, and it hit me: Not Nobbit, idiot, *Norbert!* The power of the "down east" Maine accent over the Southern/Midwestern ear! Saint Norbert was a twelfth-century reformer who ran up hard against opposition in both church and state. He fought those who heard what they wanted to hear in the gospel, putting wealth and power in front of the call to reliance on God alone. Jesus' values—with humility at the center—are different, as the widow's gift shows. Listen carefully, I've learned. Never forget that your understanding is limited and your hearing might be flawed, and in humility, be willing to correct your course and start again.

2 Timothy 4:1–8
Psalm 71:8–9,14–15ab,16–17,22
Mark 12:38–44

Sunday
JUNE 7
• THE MOST HOLY TRINITY •

God so loved the world that he gave his only Son, so that everyone who believes in him might not perish but might have eternal life.
—JOHN 3:16

To be honest, there are times in which I scoff at this whole "God is love" business. That is, as a catechetics veteran I may have been overheard noting that there are other points to teach children besides the constant drumbeat of "God loves you and you are special." But then there was that one morning several years ago in Mass. I had my arm around my sad little seven-year-old son whose daddy had died a few weeks before, and this comforting gospel was proclaimed: "God so loved the world." Isn't there more to faith than that? No, not really. No.

Exodus 34:4b–6,8–9
Daniel 3:52,53,54,55 (52b)
2 Corinthians 13:11–13
John 3:16–18

Monday
JUNE 8
• TENTH WEEK IN ORDINARY TIME •

Blessed are the poor in spirit,
for theirs is the Kingdom of Heaven.
—MATTHEW 5:3

Plunging back into Ordinary Time, we'll spend the next few months listening to Jesus, encountering him as he heals and extends mercy, and conforming our life to his. It's fitting to begin this time with the Beatitudes. As Pope Benedict XVI preached in a Vatican homily in 2006, "In truth, the blessed *par excellence* is only Jesus. He is, in fact, the true poor in spirit, the one afflicted, the meek one, the one hungering and thirsting for justice, the merciful, the pure of heart, the peacemaker. He is the one persecuted for the sake of justice." To the extent I conform my life to his, there will be my blessing, my happiness, my joy.

1 Kings 17:1–6
Psalm 121:1bc–2,3–4,5–6,7–8
Matthew 5:1–12

Just so, your light must shine before others, that they may see your good
deeds and glorify your heavenly Father.
—MATTHEW 5:16

Every night she is out there, in the same spot between a bush
and a porch post. She scuttles, sweeps, and weaves the
enormous web there in the dusk. And every morning she is
gone, along with all evidence that she was ever there at all.
I've not yet seen her catch prey, nor have I witnessed her
early morning departure. But as I watch her busy, purposeful
work, I marvel at the instinct God has given this spider and
at how she knows what to do and does it faithfully and
steadily. God has given me gifts, natural and supernatural,
through grace. When others watch me at my work, what do
they see?

1 Kings 17:7–16
Psalm 4:2–3,4–5,7b–8
Matthew 5:13–16

Wednesday

JUNE 10

Elijah appealed to all the people and said, "How long will you straddle the issue? If the LORD is God, follow him; if Baal, follow him." The people, however, did not answer him.

—1 KINGS 18:21

The prophet's words hit hard and cut deeply, even today. I don't worship Baal. But, oh, I look at my life and priorities and what I *say* I believe is true, and it's as if I'm standing right there with everyone else, listening and maybe a little shocked at what Elijah is saying. In that silence, I'll consider where I truly stand.

1 Kings 18:20–39
Psalm 16:1b–2ab,4,5ab and 8,11
Matthew 5:17–19

Thursday

JUNE 11

• ST. BARNABAS, APOSTLE •

When [Barnabas] arrived and saw the grace of God, he rejoiced and encouraged them all to remain faithful to the Lord in firmness of heart, for he was a good man, filled with the Holy Spirit and faith.

—ACTS 11:23–24

What a helpful vision for today: to enter into a situation, discern the good, and rejoice in it. There is certainly room for growth and perhaps even weeds in need of pulling, but right now, rejoice and encourage and praise God for the good that's happening here in our lives.

Acts 11:21b–26; 13:1–3
Psalm 98:1,2–3ab,3cd–4,5–6
Matthew 5:20–26

[A]fter the earthquake, there was fire—but the LORD was not in the fire.
After the fire, there was a tiny whispering sound. When he heard this,
Elijah hid his face in his cloak and went out and stood at the entrance of
the cave. A voice said to him, "Elijah, why are you here?"
—1 KINGS 19:12–13

As I begin my day, I assume that as the hours pass, certainly
I'll be attentive to the Lord. Surely it will just happen, and I'll
be present and open all day. But as the sun sets, I wonder.
Wait. What happened? Was this just one more day of
busyness and noise? The Lord is certainly speaking, but he
just might be whispering. In order to hear him, perhaps I
need to make conscious choices during the day to still myself
and listen.

1 Kings 19:9a,11–16
Psalm 27:7–8a,8b–9abc,13–14
Matthew 5:27–32

He has sent me to bring glad tidings to the lowly,
to heal the brokenhearted.
—ISAIAH 61:1

Images of St. Anthony of Padua usually show him holding
the Christ child, an allusion to one of his visions and a
symbol of the centrality of Christ in his spirituality.
Anthony's focus on Christ—that good news of God's love
that frees and heals our broken hearts—finds vivid expression
in one of his *Sermones Dominicales et Festivi* ("Sunday Sermons"),
focused this time not on the child but on the man hanging
on the cross: "If you look closely, you will be able to realize
how great your human dignity and your value are. . . .
Nowhere other than looking at himself in the mirror of the
Cross can man better understand how much he is worth."

1 Kings 19:19–21 or Isaiah 61:1–3d
Psalm 16:1b–2a,5,7–8,9–10 or 89:2–3,4–5,21–22,25,27
Matthew 5:33–37 or Luke 10:1–9

⋛ 196 ⋜

The Jews quarreled among themselves, saying, "How can this man give us his flesh to eat?" Jesus said to them, "Amen, amen, I say to you, unless you eat the flesh of the Son of Man and drink his blood, you do not have life within you."
—JOHN 6:52–53

The most thought-provoking aspect of this exchange is, quite simply, that Jesus doubles down. His questioners are understandably confused and perhaps horrified. Jesus has plenty of space and room to say anything other than what he says: What he gives to us is truly himself—all of himself. Strange, scandalous, but so deeply fitting with this human journey of seeking, desire, and hunger. We need so much, and all that we need, he gives.

Deuteronomy 8:2–3,14b–16a
Psalm 147:12–13,14–15,19–20
1 Corinthians 10:16–17
John 6:51–58

Monday

JUNE 15

*If anyone wants to go to law with you over your tunic, hand him
your cloak as well.*
—MATTHEW 5:40

Reading Jesus' words in the Sermon on the Mount, we might
be tempted to analyze, quantify, and come up with some
clear regulations. How far do we really have to walk? And
what if I only have one tunic? Do I really have to hand it
over? How many times? What a challenge it is, to discern
what a Jesus-rooted, loving response to a situation is. But the
core of the discernment, it seems to me, is always about two
words: *Let go*. Let go of pride, let go of fear, let go of
possessions, let go of the need to control. Just let go.

1 Kings 21:1–16
Psalm 5:2–3ab,4b–6a,6b–7
Matthew 5:38–42

When Ahab heard these words, he tore his garments and put on sackcloth over his bare flesh. He fasted, slept in the sackcloth, and went about subdued.
—1 KINGS 21:27

Ahab, king of Israel, received a powerful warning from God through the prophet Elisha. In response, he did the wise thing: he changed. I particularly appreciate the detail that he "went about subdued." As a person susceptible to overexplaining and justifying, I can take this to heart. Perhaps, more often than not, the best response to correction is less talk, not more.

1 Kings 21:17–29
Psalm 51:3–4,5–6ab,11,16
Matthew 5:43–48

"Take care not to perform righteous deeds in order that people may see them. . . . But when you give alms, do not let your left hand know what your right is doing, so that your almsgiving may be secret."
—MATTHEW 6:1,3–4

Several years ago we traveled on a mission trip to Mexico. A lot of preparation went into it, and the parish was constantly informed as to what we were doing before, during, and after. It was kind of a big deal. And, yes, I think we did some good. But when I came home, I couldn't help but ponder. I live in a town, in a neighborhood, even, that has people in great need. What might happen if we spent all the time and energy—and even money—that we expended on this "big" mission trip to quietly help others closer to home?

2 Kings 2:1,6–14
Psalm 31:20,21,24
Matthew 6:1–6,16–18

Thursday

JUNE 18

Then Elisha, filled with the twofold portion of his spirit,
wrought many marvels by his mere word.
During his lifetime he feared no one,
nor was any man able to intimidate his will.
—SIRACH 48:12

The prophet Elisha was gifted by God in an extraordinary way, to be sure. But even so, the same Spirit of God is offered to us, the Spirit that brings us to our knees in the presence of the Lord and brings us to our feet in the presence of worldly powers, strengthened to speak truth and testify to the power of God's love.

Sirach 48:1–14
Psalm 97:1–2,3–4,5–6,7
Matthew 6:7–15

"Come to me, all you who labor and are burdened,
and I will give you rest."
—MATTHEW 11:28

My youngest son was returning to brick-and-mortar school after living the easy homeschool life for a few years. The morning of the first day, I asked his older brother, now in high school, if he had any advice to share. Without skipping a beat, he said, "You're going to be hungry, and you're going to be tired." Kind of a succinct summation of the challenges of life—of both the material and interior life, come to think of it. That's the struggle, and Jesus enters right into it, inviting us into a place of nourishment and a place of rest: his heart.

Deuteronomy 7:6–11
Psalm 103:1–2,3–4,6–7,8,10
1 John 4:7–16
Matthew 11:25–30

Although prophets were sent to them to convert them to the LORD, the
people would not listen to their warnings.
—2 CHRONICLES 24:19

Every first Wednesday of the month around nine in the
morning, a low wailing sound fills the air in my city. It builds in
volume and seems to grow in intensity, and then it stops. It's
the tornado warning system, tested on that day every month.
In all the years I've lived here, I've only heard it once outside of
the test. At least I knew what it was and understood the
warning. When I'm straying in my spiritual journey, when I'm
in danger, I'm warned too. A sense of unease, a temptation to
pray less—it's all part of it. Will I listen?

2 Chronicles 24:17–25
Psalm 89:4–5,29–30,31–32,33–34
Luke 2:41–51

Sunday

JUNE 21

• TWELFTH SUNDAY IN ORDINARY TIME •

"What I say to you in the darkness, speak in the light; what you hear whispered, proclaim on the housetops. And do not be afraid of those who kill the body but cannot kill the soul."
—MATTHEW 10:27–28

"Don't worry what others think of you. It doesn't matter." How much energy have I spent preaching this? To my own kids, to my students, in my writing, and, yes, to myself. Always to myself. So why is it still so hard? Why is it so hard to let the Lord be all I need, his love be sufficient?

Jeremiah 20:10–13
Psalm 69:8–10,14,17,33–35 (14c)
Romans 5:12–15
Matthew 10:26–33

Monday

JUNE 22

• ST. PAULINUS OF NOLA, BISHOP • ST. JOHN FISHER, BISHOP, AND
ST. THOMAS MORE, MARTYRS •

*"Why do you notice the splinter in your brother's eye, but do not perceive
the wooden beam in your own eye? How can you say to your brother,
'Let me remove that splinter from your eye,' while the wooden beam
is in your eye?"*
—MATTHEW 7:3–4

We talk a lot about the qualities of childhood: innocence,
energy, trust. Years of parenting and being around young
people as a teacher have exposed me to another quality that
reaches peak ripeness around the age of sixteen: a hypocrisy
detector. It certainly can be irritating to hear, "But I saw
you. . . ." I admit that this eagle eye for my own inability to
practice what I preach has been essential in whatever
miniscule spiritual growth I've experienced over the decades.
Splinters and beams? They're all over. Even right here.

2 Kings 17:5–8,13–15a,18
Psalm 60:3,4–5,12–13
Matthew 7:1–5

Tuesday

JUNE 23

O God, we ponder your mercy
within your temple.
—PSALM 48:10

It's the "we" that catches me on this one. For it's true that God
calls us individually, yes, but he also calls us as a people. This
is a truth I see embodied every time I go to Mass. Whether
it's a tiny congregation during the week or a full church on
Sunday, I see it. I see the amazing variety of human beings on
this journey, seeking the Lord, bringing their pain into this
place, seeking his mercy. God is at work in every heart in
that space, reaching into every life. He is listening, healing,
and pouring out the mercy for which we all yearn.

2 Kings 19:9b–11,14–21,31–35a,36
Psalm 48:2–3ab,3cd–4,10–11
Matthew 7:6,12–14

Wednesday
JUNE 24
• THE NATIVITY OF ST. JOHN THE BAPTIST •

So they made signs, asking his father what he wished him to be called.
He asked for a tablet and wrote, "John is his name," and all were
amazed. Immediately his mouth was opened, his tongue freed, and he
spoke blessing God.
—LUKE 1:62–64

Our children are not our possessions. They're not extensions
of us, nor are they here to fulfill our dreams or expectations.
Zechariah knew this and went against all expectations in
naming his son John. Our children and all other people in
general, who might frustrate and puzzle us because they
don't fit in the box we've made for them or meet our
expectations, are who God has created and called them to
be, no matter what we think about it.

VIGIL:
Jeremiah 1:4–10
Psalm 71:1–2,3–4a,5–6ab,15ab and 17
1 Peter 1:8–12
Luke 1:5–17

DAY:
Isaiah 49:1–6
Psalm 139:1b–3,13–14ab,14c–15
Acts 13:22–26
Luke 1:57–66,80

Thursday
JUNE 25

Not everyone who says to me, "Lord, Lord," will enter the Kingdom of heaven, but only the one who does the will of my Father in heaven.
—MATTHEW 7:21

Our diocese's bishop emeritus recently passed away. At eighty-eight he had been retired for over a decade but remained quite active and independent almost until the end. My son bagged his groceries more than once during the bishop's last year. The bishop said Mass all over the diocese every weekend, preached from carefully prepared homilies, and engaged in pastoral ministry. One time our music minister ran into the bishop restocking his oils at the cathedral. He was heading to a prison to celebrate Mass and confirm some inmates—at the age of almost ninety. He was all in, not just with words but with whatever hours God had given him on this earth. Am I?

2 Kings 24:8–17
Psalm 79:1b–2,3–5,8,9
Matthew 7:21–29

Friday

JUNE 26

He stretched out his hand, touched him, and said, "I will do it.
Be made clean."
—MATTHEW 8:3

Jesus didn't have to touch the leper in order to heal him. But
he did. He reached out to him in love, reached through
prejudice and fear. There are countless ways I can share Jesus'
love with others: I can write checks, I can raise awareness, I
can support a cause. But today I'll be on the alert for a chance
to be present, to look another person in the eye, and to reach
out and through barriers with the loving touch of Christ.

2 Kings 25:1–12
Psalm 137:1–2,3,4–5,6
Matthew 8:1–4

*Jesus entered the house of Peter, and saw his mother-in-law lying in bed
with a fever. He touched her hand, the fever left her, and she rose and
waited on him.*
—MATTHEW 8:14–15

Sometimes it seems as if this journey is a cycle. We take life
for granted for a time; then we're shocked out of
complacency by something delightful or tragic; and then
we're lulled right back into inattention and narrowness of
vision. I may not have been raised from a sickbed by the
direct touch of Jesus, but he has moved me and healed me.
He has even startled me out of the ordinary and opened my
eyes and given me new life. What a loss it is when even for a
day—even for an hour—I slip back into forgetting.

Lamentations 2:2,10–14,18–19
Psalm 74:1b–2,3–5,6–7,20–21
Matthew 8:5–17

If, then, we have died with Christ, we believe that we shall also live with him. We know that Christ, raised from the dead, dies no more; death no longer has power over him.

—ROMANS 6:8–9

Death has no power over Jesus. And we, descended into the tomb via the waters of baptism, we rise with him, and it has no power over us either. Driving by a cemetery and suddenly seized with anxiety, remembering and missing people I love who have died, considering tragedy after tragedy that I hear about through the news, I have to keep remembering Paul's words to the Romans, praying over them, and letting them take root, grow, and overpower my fears:
Death no longer has power.

2 Kings 4:8–11,14–16a
Psalm 89:2–3,16–17,18–19 (2a)
Romans 6:3–4,8–11
Matthew 10:37–42

Monday

JUNE 29

*I, Paul, am already being poured out like a libation, and the time of my
departure is at hand. I have competed well; I have finished the race;
I have kept the faith.*
—2 TIMOTHY 4:6–7

Peter: a fisherman tending his nets with his brother on the
Sea of Galilee. Paul: a learned man of faith working in
opposition to the Way. Both called by Jesus himself, both
changed, transformed and empowered in that unexpected,
even shocking way that God has of doing things. Their
stories remind me over and over again: Take the risk to be
open, be ready for God to use you—yes, even you—in
surprising ways.

VIGIL:
Acts 3:1–10
Psalm 19:2–3,4–5
Galatians 1:11–20
John 21:15–19

DAY:
Acts 12:1–11
Psalm 34:2–3,4–5,6–7,8–9
2 Timothy 4:6–8,17–18
Matthew 16:13–19

Tuesday

JUNE 30

He said to them, "Why are you terrified, O you of little faith?"
—MATTHEW 8:26

One of the greatest obstacles in my writing life is fear. Not of how my writing will be received, but simply of the size and scope of a project and my abilities, so inadequate to the task. Why even start? The other day I was working on a fiction piece. I sat there, paralyzed. And then I thought, "I don't have to write the Great American Novel (or story) in the next fifteen minutes. All I have to do is describe this chicken." (It was an egg cup shaped like a chicken.) So it is today. I don't have to save the world or fix all the problems. I am just called to love the person in front of me, let Jesus in a bit more, and not be afraid.

Amos 3:1–8; 4:11–12
Psalm 5:4b–6a,6b–7,8
Matthew 8:23–27

Wednesday

JULY 1

• ST. JUNIPERO SERRA, PRIEST •

Away with your noisy songs!
I will not listen to the melodies of your harps.
But if you would offer me burnt offerings,
then let justice surge like water,
and goodness like an unfailing stream.
—AMOS 5:23–24

The problems of this world and the profound sufferings of others can be overwhelming. What is our responsibility? How, indeed, can we celebrate in the comfort of our safe, secure spaces when so much injustice abounds? Our responses will vary according to our own gifts and circumstances, but it certainly starts here, every day: listen to the prophets, beware of complacency, and admit that, no, everything is not okay.

Amos 5:14–15,21–24
Psalm 50:7,8–9,10–11,12–13,16bc–17
Matthew 8:28–34

And there people brought to him a paralytic lying on a stretcher. When Jesus saw their faith, he said to the paralytic, "Courage, child, your sins are forgiven."

—MATTHEW 9:2

How does Jesus prepare this man for healing and mercy? By telling him to have courage. Why courage, I wonder? To start living in a way that's free from the excuses we tend to make when we're bound down by sinful habits ("That's just the way it is"; "That's who I am"), to let God take those away and start again. To stand up and become healed people. Well, that takes courage.

Amos 7:10–17
Psalm 19:8,9,10,11
Matthew 9:1–8

Friday

JULY 3

• ST. THOMAS, APOSTLE •

Then he said to Thomas, "Put your finger here and see my hands, and
bring your hand and put it into my side."
—JOHN 20:27

A long time ago my son stumbled into the open dishwasher
door. A knife stupidly put sharp side up in the cutlery rack
stabbed his leg. Twenty years later you can still see the scar. I
glance at my forearm and a darkened crescent shape reminds
me of the time when I burned myself with an iron. Our scars
are evidence of adventures or mistakes. They also can be
signs of surprising strength. We recognize ourselves in part
through our scars, the signs of our wounds. Thomas was in
Jesus' presence but held back, hesitant—until he touched the
wound in Jesus' side. In and through these wounds, he
remembered, he recognized, he understood.

Ephesians 2:19–22
Psalm 117:1bc,2
John 20:24–29

⇒ 216 ⇐

Saturday

JULY 4

• INDEPENDENCE DAY •

*"People do not put new wine into old wineskins. Otherwise the skins
burst, the wine spills out, and the skins are ruined. Rather, they pour new
wine into fresh wineskins, and both are preserved."*
—MATTHEW 9:17

Christmas break of my freshman year in college was a
challenging time. Even those first three months away from
home had changed me. As my own children grow and
encounter new circumstances, I see the same dynamic at
work. It's amazing to think that every person I know is
continually being engaged in new ways. I don't always see
these changes. People look mostly the same on the outside
day after day. But who knows what new wine has been
poured into their souls? Jesus' words are one more reminder:
Be open to the possibility and power of the new, not just in
ourselves but in others' lives as well.

Amos 9:11–15
Psalm 85:9ab,10,11–12,13–14
Matthew 9:14–17

"Come to me, all you who labor and are burdened, and I will give you rest. Take my yoke upon you and learn from me, for I am meek and humble of heart; and you will find rest for yourselves."
—MATTHEW 11:28–30

My youngest son is fascinated by ancient American histories, so we've spent a good deal of time studying and visiting sites associated with the Maya, Aztec, and other cultures. With every encounter I'm struck by the contrast between the harshness of so many ancient pagan religions and the words of Jesus. What a light Jesus' gentle words must have been, but what a pity that so often Jesus' comforting words are obscured by those called to share it, even as missionaries. Obscured not just by institutions past and present but by me, too.

Zechariah 9:9–10
Psalm 145:1–2,8–9,10–11,13–14
Romans 8:9,11–13
Matthew 11:25–30

Monday
JULY 6
• ST. MARIA GORETTI, VIRGIN AND MARTYR •

When Jesus arrived at the official's house and saw the flute players and the crowd who were making a commotion, he said, "Go away! The girl is not dead but sleeping." And they ridiculed him.
—MATTHEW 9:23–24

In the day that has just passed and the new day coming soon, problems lurk. Will I let those problems overpower and threaten me, or will I listen to Jesus? Will I allow him to help me see things as they really are, dismiss the noisemakers in my head, and open the door to his healing presence?

Hosea 2:16,17b–18,21–22
Psalm 145:2–3,4–5,6–7,8–9
Matthew 9:18–26

Their idols are silver and gold,
the handiwork of men.
They have mouths but speak not;
they have eyes but see not.
—PSALM 115:4–5

Over the past few years, controversies have erupted about statues and other signs of honor. People in a past era might have believed a particular historical figure worthy of honor; today, circumstances past and present make honoring them problematic. Statues have been pulled down, buildings renamed, celebrations erased. I am not a fan of targeted forgetting or pretending the past didn't happen, but each time something like this happens, I wonder if the problem goes deeper. Perhaps they're all idols of some sort, and our first mistake was erecting and honoring statues of flawed, sinful human beings at all.

Hosea 8:4–7,11–13
Psalm 115:3–4,5–6,7ab–8,9–10
Matthew 9:32–38

Wednesday
July 8

Jesus sent out these Twelve after instructing them thus, "Do not go into pagan territory or enter a Samaritan town. Go rather to the lost sheep of the house of Israel. As you go, make this proclamation: 'The kingdom of heaven is at hand.'"
—MATTHEW 10:5–7

We are so accustomed to thinking about Jesus reaching out to the excluded and the outcast (the Samaritan being such a powerful symbol of that) that these words are surprising.

Upon reflection, though, they simply indicate that for everything, there is, indeed, a season. There are no rules for outreach, only discernment. We must continually be open to be led by Jesus to share his love in the places and times and ways he may lead us.

Hosea 10:1–3,7–8,12
Psalm 105:2–3,4–5,6–7
Matthew 10:1–7

Thursday

JULY 9

• ST. AUGUSTINE ZHAO RONG, PRIEST, AND COMPANIONS, MARTYRS •

I drew them with human cords,
with bands of love;
I fostered them like one
who raises an infant to his cheeks;
Yet though I stopped to feed my child,
they did not know that I was their healer.
—HOSEA 11:4

What a striking image this Scripture gives us. The Lord teaching us, holding us, treasuring us—and we, like small children, knowing the love but unaware of who it is who cares for us so deeply. It's an image of the God who created each of us out of gracious, astonishing love, and whose care sustains us every hour of every day—right now.

Hosea 11:1–4,8e–9
Psalm 80:2ac,3b,15–16
Matthew 10:7–15

Friday

JULY 10

*We shall say no more, "Our god,"
to the work of our hands.*
—HOSEA 14:4

If I believe I can't be happy without "it," if my sense of self
depends on it, if I'm sure that everything would be all right if
I just had it in my life, then "it" is like a god to me. And if it is
in any way shaped or formed by human hands, then it won't
do what I think it will or satisfy any need. Not now, not ever,
and certainly not forever.

Hosea 14:2–10
Psalm 51:3–4,8–9,12–13,14,17
Matthew 10:16–23

⇒ 223 ⇐

"What I say to you in the darkness, speak in the light; what you hear whispered, proclaim on the housetops."
—MATTHEW 10:27

How many times has it happened? I know I should say something. Maybe it's an idea I have, or an observation that might help someone correct course, or a word that might offer comfort. Too often I'm hesitant or even afraid to speak up. And, yes, there is a time to speak and a time to be silent. But when it is time, when the moment calls for it, when I've discerned this is where the Lord wants me to be so I can speak, then digging deep and opening up to the Spirit, I pray for courage to obey.

Isaiah 6:1–8
Psalm 93:1ab,1cd–2,5
Matthew 10:24–33

Sunday

JULY 12

• FIFTEENTH SUNDAY IN ORDINARY TIME •

For creation awaits with eager expectation the revelation of the children of God . . . in hope that creation itself would be set free from slavery to corruption and share in the glorious freedom of the children of God.
—ROMANS 8:19–21

Well, that's sad. Just yesterday we could see the baby robins' heads popping up from their nest under the eaves next to the patio. This morning, the nest was on the ground, torn to bits, surrounded by feathers and little legs, and the parent birds sat on the cable wire above me, chirping plaintively. I'm assuming it was a hawk's work. I admit that the cruelty one finds in nature challenges me. Paul alerts me to hope: hope that in Christ, one day all the cruelty—animal and human (ours tragically, freely chosen)—will be redeemed and the tears shed because of it will be wiped away.

Isaiah 55:10–11
Psalm 65:10,11,12–13,14
Romans 8:18–23
Matthew 13:1–23 or 13:1–9

⇒ 225 ⇐

Monday
JULY 13
• ST. HENRY •

"[W]hoever loves son or daughter more than me is not worthy of me; and whoever does not take up his cross and follow after me is not worthy of me."
—MATTHEW 10:37–38

In 1639, Sr. Marie de l'Incarnation left France for Canada, where she spent the rest of her life ministering to the indigenous peoples. But she left more than her country: she left a son whom she never saw again. They did correspond, and in *From Mother to Son* she writes in a letter: "When I left you, you were not twelve years old and I did so only with strange agonies known to God alone. I had to obey his divine will, which wanted things to happen thus, making me hope that he would take care of you." A radical path, certainly, that might not inspire imitation, but it can inspire reflection on our priorities and choices.

Isaiah 1:10–17
Psalm 50:8–9,16bc–17,21,23
Matthew 10:34—11:1

Tuesday

JULY 14

• ST. KATERI TEKAKWITHA, VIRGIN •

Jesus began to reproach the towns where most of his mighty deeds had been done, since they had not repented.
—MATTHEW 11:20

It is so important to keep the Lord's mercy, love, and acceptance at the center of my day. Jesus moves through my life, too, working mighty deeds. What has been my response? Have I repented? Have I said yes to his presence and his love? Or do I persist in holding back my entire heart?

Isaiah 7:1–9
Psalm 48:2–3a,3b–4,5–6,7–8
Matthew 11:20–24

Wednesday

JULY 15

Shall he who shaped the ear not hear?
or he who formed the eye not see?
—PSALM 94:9

I don't have nearly as many anxiety dreams as I used to, but when I do, they share the same setting as they always have. I'm in the classroom, either as a student or a teacher, totally unprepared to either take or give an exam. What a relief it is to realize later that it was, indeed, only a dream. Sometimes my waking life can be filled with different sorts of anxiety and worry. Reading the psalms can be so comforting in those times. What a relief it is when I realize that God sees and hears all! The fear that I am in this all alone is, indeed, nothing but a dream.

Isaiah 10:5–7,13b–16
Psalm 94:5–6,7–8,9–10,14–15
Matthew 11:25–27

Thursday

JULY 16

• OUR LADY OF MOUNT CARMEL •

My soul yearns for you in the night,
yes, my spirit within me keeps vigil for you.
—ISAIAH 26:9

In Christ so much is revealed—mercy, truth, life, and the
nature of God's love for us. But do we know everything? Not
quite. Life still courses with mystery, and we still look into
the night and keep vigil in the dawn, wondering, musing,
seeking answers. A man in my parish, recently diagnosed
with Parkinson's disease, offered a clue of how to live with
this mystery through thought-provoking words the pastor
reprinted in the bulletin: "God has a right to his secrets."

Isaiah 26:7–9,12,16–19
Psalm 102:13–14ab,15,16–18,19–21
Matthew 11:28–30

⇒ 229 ⇐

You have folded up my life, like a weaver
who severs the last thread.
—ISAIAH 38:12

I looked pretty much the same for about twenty years. For a few years now (as you read this, I'm turning sixty), things have obviously been changing. General good health had also contributed to that assumption of agelessness. Well, I don't feel ageless anymore. I don't feel decrepit, but at the same time, the earthly future doesn't feel limitless any longer either. This aging business has a way of reordering one's thinking and adjusting priorities. Of course, God has been telling me all along what really matters. I can't deny mortality, but listening to his promises, I can't deny them either. As my body sinks lower toward the ground, ironically, I might just be more disposed to raise my spirit to him and listen.

Isaiah 38:1–6,21–22,7–8
Isaiah 38:10,11,12abcd,16
Matthew 12:1–8

Saturday

JULY 18

• ST. CAMILLUS DE LELLIS, PRIEST •

[F]or you behold misery and sorrow,
taking them in your hands.
On you the unfortunate man depends;
of the fatherless you are the helper.
—PSALM 10:14

If you want a compelling story of mercy and conversion, you can't do much better than St. Camillus de Lellis. A soldier of fortune and a gambler with a bad temper, Camillus would be the last person you'd expect to found a religious order devoted to care of the sick and wounded. But after a conversion experience and rejection by other orders, that's exactly what he did, and the Camillians still minister today. No matter who we are, God can use us. No matter how badly wounded we are, God can heal us and use our hands to reach out to the sorrowful.

Micah 2:1–5
Psalm 10:1–2,3–4,7–8,14
Matthew 12:14–21

Sunday

JULY 19

• SIXTEENTH SUNDAY IN ORDINARY TIME •

*The Spirit comes to the aid of our weakness; for we do not know
how to pray as we ought.*
—ROMANS 8:26

How true this Scripture is. It's not that I don't know the right
words. No, it's that in the narrowness of my vision I really
don't know what I should be praying for. I may think I know
what's best for me, those I care about, and even the whole
world, but do I? That's why the words the Spirit gives me
through the church are so important. Through them, even
when I don't want to forgive or see others at peace, I pray for
it. When I don't feel any need to be humble, the psalms, for
example, plant my feet on the ground and position me in my
right relation to God. Through all of these ancient and
well-worn prayers, my spirit is formed, and I learn
how to pray.

Wisdom 12:13,16–19
Psalm 86:5–6,9–10,15–16 (5a)
Romans 8:26–27
Matthew 13:24–43 or 13:24–30

[T]here is something greater than Jonah here.
—MATTHEW 12:41

So much of the Gospel narrative is about seeing and recognizing. Or, more accurately, the lack of it. Jesus was right there with his disciples, but did they even have a clue? Usually not. It's a good corrective for me in the times I might be tempted to use the distance of two thousand years as a reason to complain and doubt: "If only I'd been there to see Jesus in person, it would be so much easier to believe." Over and over I see that's not the case. There's something else in the way. It's up to me to be honest about that. It's up to me to humbly discern what's standing in the way of my recognition of the One who has, indeed, promised to be with me always.

Micah 6:1–4,6–8
Psalm 50:5–6,8–9,16bc–17,21,23
Matthew 12:38–42

Tuesday

JULY 21

• ST. LAWRENCE OF BRINDISI, PRIEST AND DOCTOR OF THE CHURCH •

You will cast into the depths of the sea all our sins.
—MICAH 7:19

Who am I? What defines me? Am I God's beloved child or have I become convinced that I am defined by my sins, flaws, and failures? Pride takes different forms. Might one of them be visible as we stand at the shores of the sea, clinging to that baggage we're convinced is just too heavy for God to take from us—and fling into the sea?

Micah 7:14–15,18–20
Psalm 85:2–4,5–6,7–8
Matthew 12:46–50

Jesus said to her, "Mary!"
—JOHN 20:16

Mary Magdalene, healed of demon possession, responds to
Jesus with a life of faithful discipleship. As spiritual writers
and theologians will point out, she's like the bride in the
Song of Songs. She's like the church itself, called by Christ
out of bondage to the evils that pervade our world, waiting
with hope by the tomb, even when all seems lost.

Song of Songs 3:1–4b or 2 Corinthians 5:14–17
Psalm 71:1–2,3–4a,5–6ab,15,17
John 20:1–2,11–18

Thursday

JULY 23

• ST. BRIDGET, RELIGIOUS •

For with you is the fountain of life,
and in your light we see light.
—PSALM 36:10

What is it we want to see? Plants and animals? Rivers, forests, and the stars? Other human beings? Certainly. In the glow of created light, we can see the world in this way. But our hearts yearn for an even deeper kind of seeing. We long to understand our place in the world now and to know that our heavenly destination is impossible to miss. Here with the Lord, in the light of his love, all of this we can finally see.

Jeremiah 2:1–3,7–8,12–13
Psalm 36:6–7ab,8–9,10–11
Matthew 13:10–17

Friday
JULY 24

"But the seed sown on rich soil is the one who hears the word and understands it, who indeed bears fruit and yields a hundred or sixty or thirtyfold."
—MATTHEW 13:23

The first time I visited Mexico, I noticed a statue of a saint unfamiliar to me in several churches. Dressed in a monastic habit, the statues often were festooned with ribbons. It turns out it was St. Sharbel Makhlūf. He's very popular in Mexico. He was a Maronite Catholic who never left Lebanon and had a reputation for deep holiness. His popularity in Mexico is due in part to a substantial Lebanese population, but also, I like to think, simply because of what happens when the seed of the gospel is planted anywhere. It bears fruit, a hundred or sixty or thirtyfold.

Jeremiah 3:14–17
Jeremiah 31:10,11–12abcd,13
Matthew 13:18–23

Saturday

JULY 25

• ST. JAMES, APOSTLE •

We hold this treasure in earthen vessels, that the surpassing power may
be of God and not from us. We are afflicted in every way,
but not constrained.
—2 CORINTHIANS 4:7–8

One Saturday in October, my two youngest sons and I
joined dozens of others in a parking lot dotted with huge
bins of sweet potatoes. Our task? To bag up the tubers
collected by this gleaning group for distribution to the
needy. In response to my son's question, I explained that
these potatoes were too oddly shaped, large, or small to be
sold in stores. They were imperfect—"weak." Paul's letters
resound with the truth of his experience. The world may
celebrate strength and perfection, but Paul knows that
natural weakness doesn't stop God; in fact, it's the opposite.
In our weakness, God's love can be most powerfully shown
and shared with an aching, hungry world.

2 Corinthians 4:7–15
Psalm 126:1bc–2ab,2cd–3,4–5,6
Matthew 20:20–28

⇒ 238 ⇐

Sunday

JULY 26

• SEVENTEENTH SUNDAY IN ORDINARY TIME •

We know that all things work for good for those who love God.
—ROMANS 8:28

On the afternoon before my husband's funeral, my daughter bought a dress she'd seen in the window of a vintage clothing store. Prom was coming in a few weeks, and life does go on. It was a 1950s faux-Asian style in a brilliant, shimmering green. As she walked into the hotel room wearing it, I thought, *She looks different—because Mike died.* Later, a younger friend's husband died in a car accident. She eventually remarried and had a baby, a child who wouldn't have existed if her heart had not been shattered by a midnight visit from a state trooper. What can we do with this mystery of the interplay of beauty and tragedy, joy and sorrow at the heart of life? Only God knows. Only God.

1 Kings 3:5,7–12
Psalm 119:57,72,76–77,127–128,129–130 (97a)
Romans 8:28–30
Matthew 13:44–52 or 13:44–46

⇒ 239 ⇐

*The Kingdom of heaven is like a mustard seed that a person took and
sowed in a field. It is the smallest of all the seeds, yet when full-grown
it is the largest of plants.*
—MATTHEW 13:31–32

Isn't it strange how we don't notice growth or gradual
change? When we're living every day with a child, he or she
always seems the same. That full-grown adult is quite
different from the baby—how did that happen? Growth in
faith can be sudden, upending our lives and vision.
Sometimes that growth is more gradual and may even
frustrate us because we can't see it. If we look back honestly
(perhaps with feedback from others who know us well), we
can see that we have changed: imperceptibly but surely,
Christ's love has taken root and in quiet but sure ways,
flourished.

Jeremiah 13:1–11
Deuteronomy 32:18–19,20,21
Matthew 13:31–35

Tuesday

JULY 28

Among the nations' idols is there any that give rain?
Or can the mere heavens send showers?
Is it not you alone, O LORD,
our God, to whom we look?
You alone have done all these things.
—JEREMIAH 14:22

Jeremiah speaks to the people in the midst of a drought, challenging them to reflect on the solutions they're seeking. How pointless it is to turn to these idols, these pretend remedies that can do nothing, he says. There are all kinds of droughts, all kinds of problems that beset us. It's good to listen to the prophet and take an honest look at what we've settled on as a solution. Is it rooted in the Lord's power and will, or is it simply an idol that has no real power, only the hopes we've invested in it?

Jeremiah 14:17–22
Psalm 79:8,9,11,13
Matthew 13:36–43

Wednesday

JULY 29

• ST. MARTHA •

Jesus told her, "I am the resurrection and the life; whoever believes in me, even if he dies, will live, and everyone who lives and believes in me will never die. Do you believe this?" She said to him, "Yes, Lord. I have come to believe that you are the Christ, the Son of God, the one who is coming into the world."
—JOHN 11:25–27

Martha encounters Jesus in the midst of crisis and grief. In that moment, they have a conversation. A dialogue. She's honest with Jesus. She holds nothing back. And in that honest dialogue with the Lord, Martha finds hope.

Jeremiah 15:10,16–21
Psalm 59:2–3,4,10–11,17,18
John 11:19–27 or Luke 10:38–42

Thursday
JULY 30

• ST. PETER CHRYSOLOGUS, BISHOP AND DOCTOR OF THE CHURCH •

This word came to Jeremiah from the LORD: Rise up, be off to the potter's house; there I will give you my message. I went down to the potter's house and there he was, working at the wheel.

—JEREMIAH 18:1–3

Part of me wants to stay where I am, to sit tight and stay put. But there's that nudge, that push, that persistent voice that says, *Get out of the house, step through that bubble, open your eyes, and listen.* In what strange, unexpected but perfectly ordinary place will the Lord show up today?

Jeremiah 18:1–6
Psalm 146:1b–2,3–4,5–6ab
Matthew 13:47–53

*And he did not work many mighty deeds there because of their
lack of faith.*
—MATTHEW 13:58

What is faith? It is trust. This spiritual dynamic isn't about
intellectual assent to a correct definition. It's about trusting in
the Lord's power and love. We never know what fruit we
might see if we simply opened up and trusted Jesus more.
Change can happen when we have faith in his mighty deeds.

Jeremiah 26:1–9
Psalm 69:5,8–10,14
Matthew 13:54–58

*"As for me, I am in your hands; do with me what is good and right. . . .
[I]t was the LORD who sent me to you, to speak all these things for
you to hear."*
—JEREMIAH 26:14–15

St. Alphonsus Liguori wrote on many subjects in his letters,
including practical matters related to his books. Quite often,
he's aggravated: "If I could only visit Naples, I might be able
to do something personally. But confined here in this
poverty-stricken Arienzo, I write letters innumerable to
people in Naples about the sale, but with very little result. I
am much afflicted at this, but affliction seems to be all that I
am to reap from these negotiations." Even the saints, it
seems, meet obstacles and uncertainty as they speak the
words the Lord has called them to share with a
skeptical world.

Jeremiah 26:11–16,24
Psalm 69:15–16,30–31,33–34
Matthew 14:1–12

Thus says the LORD:
All you who are thirsty,
come to the water!
You who have no money,
come, receive grain and eat.
—ISAIAH 55:1

From time to time we volunteer to help serve meals at a local shelter. It's always a smooth, positive experience, but I admit to feeling awkward at times. I have a constant running monologue in my head that goes something like this: "Please don't think that I think I am superior to you because I'm serving and you're receiving. Will you take my smile as a friendly smile or a condescending one? But if I don't smile, what will you think?" Ultimately I just have to trust. I have to be myself, share what I have, and never forget about my own poverty and the many ways I end up being served by others every day.

Isaiah 55:1–3
Psalm 145:8–9,15–16,17–18
Romans 8:35,37–39
Matthew 14:13–21

When the disciples saw him walking on the sea they were terrified. "It is a ghost," they said, and they cried out in fear. At once Jesus spoke to them, "Take courage, it is I; do not be afraid."
—MATTHEW 14:26–27

What appears in front of me might seem frightening. But is there a chance that this mystery I'm facing is really a space where the Lord lives and that he's beckoning me to approach him in trust?

Jeremiah 28:1–17
Psalm 119:29,43,79,80,95,102
Matthew 14:22–36

Tuesday

AUGUST 4

*Then his disciples approached and said to him, "Do you know that the
Pharisees took offense when they heard what you said?" He said in reply,
"Every plant that my heavenly Father has not planted will be uprooted.
Let them alone; they are blind guides of the blind. If a blind man leads a
blind man, both will fall into a pit."*
—MATTHEW 15:12–14

Jesus teaches us to reach out, to love boldly, to sacrifice, and
to be light and salt for the earth. He also teaches us to let go.
It can be hard to respect people's freedom, and it can be
distressing to let people live with their mistakes. But we love,
we do what we can, and we pray. As hard as it is, we might
just have to listen in sorrow and acceptance to Jesus' words
here: "Let them alone."

Jeremiah 30:1–2,12–15,18–22
Psalm 102:16–18,19–21,29,22–23
Matthew 14:22–36 or 15:1–2,10–14

I will turn their mourning into joy.
I will console and gladden them after their sorrows.
—JEREMIAH 31:13

My son was in a piano lesson on a college campus. I was waiting in a college classroom building as classes changed. One by one, students walked by, read a notice on the classroom door, and then jumped around and shouted things like "Praise the Lord!" (It was a Baptist school.) The test they'd expected had been postponed. I know that the kind of joy the Lord offers is about much more than relief over a delayed exam. But the fact that their celebrations brought a smile to the face of a stranger waiting in the corner was a reminder to me of the power of joy, period, and how easy it is to share it—even unawares.

Jeremiah 31:1–7
Jeremiah 31:10,11–12ab,13
Matthew 15:21–28

Thursday

AUGUST 6

• THE TRANSFIGURATION OF THE LORD •

We did not follow cleverly devised myths when we made known to you
the power and coming of our Lord Jesus Christ, but we had been
eyewitnesses of his majesty.
—2 PETER 1:16

Eyewitnesses. The gift of faith we've been given is all because of witnesses. The apostles and other friends of Jesus not only stood on the mountain seeing his glory but also heard him speak, saw him heal, watched him die, and shared food with him after he rose from the dead. Their witness was passed on through preachers and teachers and in the simplicity and richness of women teaching their children prayers at the fireside. This is true! Jesus is Lord, and through him there is mercy and life eternal. We've seen; we've heard; and now we share that good news.

Daniel 7:9–10,13–14
Psalm 97:1–2,5–6,9 (1a,9a)
2 Peter 1:16–19
Matthew 17:1–9

*[W]hoever wishes to save his life will lose it, but whoever loses his life for
my sake will find it.*
—MATTHEW 16:25

One day at Mass the priest chanted the Gospel. It was
unexpected, and it got my attention. After decades of hearing
Jesus' words, often I take them for granted. I half listen and
let my mind move on to other things, even with words as
radical as these of Jesus echoing in my ear. Hearing the
Gospel chanted that morning prompted me to take notice
and to listen in a new way. Perhaps that is something I should
try to do more often.

Nahum 2:1,3; 3:1–3,6–7
Deuteronomy 32:35cd–36ab,39abcd,41
Matthew 16:24–28

Saturday

AUGUST 8

• ST. DOMINIC, PRIEST •

For the vision still has its time,
presses on to fulfillment, and will not disappoint.
—HABAKKUK 2:3

The Lord lives. He is present. He guides and comforts. In the
face of loss and limitations, questions and worry, hold on and
listen to the promise. He will not disappoint. The Lord lives.

Habakkuk 1:12—2:4
Psalm 9:8–9,10–11,12–13
Matthew 17:14–20

*I speak the truth in Christ, I do not lie; my conscience joins with the
Holy Spirit in bearing me witness that I have great sorrow and constant
anguish in my heart.*
—ROMANS 9:1–2

Does faithful discipleship mean being happy all the time?
Not if by *happy* we mean it in a superficial sense that ignores
the difficult realities of life. Here, Paul expresses his sadness
about his experience of the people of God's closedness to the
Good News he is preaching. It was a burden and a mystery
to him, and not something he could gloss over with a cheery
grin. But what he could do is hand the mystery over to the
Lord who'd called him.

1 Kings 19:9a,11–13a
Psalm 85:9,10,11–12,13–14
Romans 9:1–5
Matthew 14:22–33

Monday

AUGUST 10

• ST. LAWRENCE, DEACON AND MARTYR •

Whoever serves me must follow me, and where I am, there also will my servant be. The Father will honor whoever serves me.
—JOHN 12:26

My son and I sat in the darkened monastery church. Other than the figures in the striking mid-century wall murals, we were alone. Finally, the monks trickled in and settled in their stalls, and Compline began. Not one of them paid us any mind except for a monk who caught my eye. He subtly motioned for us to join them in line for the Abbot's night blessing. It was satisfying, a useful corrective to the temptation to approach my spiritual journey as a consumer, expecting to have my needs met by an institution or organization. I, too, am a disciple, called to serve, not to be served, and that night the call came to serve the Lord in grateful, quiet worship.

2 Corinthians 9:6–10
Psalm 112:1–2,5–6,7–8,9
John 12:24–26

Tuesday

AUGUST 11

• ST. CLARE, VIRGIN •

In the way of your decrees I rejoice,
as much as in all riches.
—PSALM 119:14

Of the very few writings St. Clare left behind, the most
substantive are four letters to Agnes of Bohemia, a princess
who joined the Poor Clares. What I love about these letters
is that Clare engages Agnes by using familiar imagery from
Agnes's life of privilege: jewels, adornment, marriage, and
even mirrors. At that time only a wealthy person would have
had a mirror, and Clare uses it as a way to describe Christ.
With Christ as our mirror, we look and see not ourselves but
him: "Indeed, blessed poverty, holy humility, and ineffable
charity are reflected in that mirror," she writes. She met
Agnes where she was, trusting that in that place, she would
hear Christ's call to draw closer to him.

Ezekiel 2:8—3:4
Psalm 119:14,24,72,103,111,131
Matthew 18:1–5,10,12–14

Wednesday

AUGUST 12

• ST. JANE FRANCES DE CHANTAL, RELIGIOUS •

*Praise, you servants of the LORD,
praise the name of the LORD.*
—PSALM 113:1

One of St. Jane de Chantal's great concerns was to encourage those she guided to center their energies on the Lord in praise, gratitude, and obedience rather than in constant self-examination, which can, if we're not careful, become an endless exercise in vanity. In a letter to Sr. Marie Aimée de Blonay in 1616, she writes, "Indeed, as much may be said of this fault of over-sensitiveness. Pray what does it matter whether you are dense and stolid or over-sensitive? Any one can see that all this is simply self-love seeking its satisfaction. For the love of God let me hear no more of it: love your own insignificance and the most holy will of God which has allotted it to you."

Ezekiel 9:1–7; 10:18–22
Psalm 113:1–2,3–4,5–6
Matthew 18:15–20

I did as I was told. During the day I brought out my baggage as though it were that of an exile, and at evening I dug a hole through the wall with my hand and, while they looked on, set out in the darkness, shouldering my burden.

—EZEKIEL 12:7

God calls Ezekiel to use quite a dramatic gesture here to get his point across to his rebellious people. Likewise, in today's Gospel, Jesus tells the dramatic parable of the unforgiving debtor who must pay a high price for his hypocrisy and lack of mercy. Sometimes the routine and relative ease of ordinary life lull me into complacency. Reflecting on what Ezekiel and Jesus are saying and how they are saying it, I'm jolted out of that complacency. Life is a profound gift. Do my choices reflect a deep awareness of that gift and the possible consequences of misusing it or even taking it for granted?

Ezekiel 12:1–12
Psalm 78:56–57,58–59,61–62
Matthew 18:21—19:1

Friday

AUGUST 14

• ST. MAXIMILIAN KOLBE, PRIEST AND MARTYR •

God is indeed my savior;
I am confident and unafraid.
—ISAIAH 12:2

This verse is certainly worth memorizing and carrying around with me during the day. Who knows what I'll face today or tomorrow? Who knows what I'll be called to do or say that might lead me far beyond my comfort zone or into unknown territory? With the words of Isaiah on my lips—and more important, in my heart—perhaps I can meet whatever comes with the kind of courage and grace that comes only from the Lord.

Ezekiel 16:1–15,60,63 or 16:59–63
Isaiah 12:2–3,4bcd,5–6
Matthew 19:3–12

AUGUST 15

• THE ASSUMPTION OF THE BLESSED VIRGIN MARY •

He has shown the strength of his arm,
and has scattered the proud in their conceit.
He has cast down the mighty from their thrones,
and has lifted up the lowly.
—LUKE 1:51–52

When I consider the life of this young woman from Galilee, one word springs to mind: *hope*. In her and through her "yes," hope took root in a world damaged by sin. Hope for our brokenness, hope for a scarred world, hope for all of us. Laid low by fear of the specter of death, a darkness that seems mighty and overwhelming and powerful enough to rob us of all joy, we witness God's work in Mary's life, and we see, hear, and sing with her: *Hope.*

VIGIL:
1 Chronicles 15:3–4,15–16; 16:1–2
Psalm 132:6–7,9–10,13–14
1 Corinthians 15:54b–57
Luke 11:27–28

DAY:
Revelation 11:19a; 12:1–6a,10ab
Psalm 45:10,11,12,16
1 Corinthians 15:20–27
Luke 1:39–56

Sunday

AUGUST 16

• TWENTIETH SUNDAY IN ORDINARY TIME •

*Them I will bring to my holy mountain
and make them joyful in my house of prayer.*
—ISAIAH 56:7

It might be tempting to attend Mass and experience it as a spectator or even a critic. I have that tendency, I admit. But it's important that we set that aside and try to see others through the eyes of faith, as children of a loving God doing the best they can. As we all bow before the holiness of the Lord, we will find joy here together in this house of prayer.

Isaiah 56:1,6–7
Psalm 67:2–3,5,6,8
Romans 11:13–15,29–32
Matthew 15:21–28

AUGUST 17

Jesus said to him, "If you wish to be perfect, go, sell what you have and give to the poor, and you will have treasure in heaven. Then come, follow me."
—MATTHEW 19:21

We traveled to the site of Alabama's first state capital—Old Cahawba. The town flourished until after the Civil War, when the railroads shifted away and the inhabitants packed up and left. Almost two hundred years later, it consists of a swamp, groves of live oak trees, and a few chimneys. As we walked amid the silent emptiness, my first thoughts ran along the usual melancholy-in-the-ruins theme, centered on what was gone. But then another angle struck me: the flexibility, freedom, and courage it takes to respond to reality—the most "real" reality being not political or social but the voice of the Lord himself calling us to follow—and just pack up our fears and go.

Ezekiel 24:15–24
Deuteronomy 32:18–19,20,21
Matthew 19:16–22

Jesus looked at them and said, "For men this is impossible, but for God all things are possible."
—MATTHEW 19:26

Dreams can be mysterious and odd and can stick with you. More often than I can say, I am stopped short midmorning by a vivid and complete recollection of a dream I had forgotten until that moment. It's so weird. It's a good reminder of how little I understand about life and even about myself. There is more, much more than meets the eye. There are layers, heights, and depths. That truth could be frightening, but it's not. None of it is an accident, because the Lord creates and sustains in mystery, yes, but also with love and eternal possibility.

Ezekiel 28:1–10
Deuteronomy 32:26–27ab,27cd–28,30,35cd–36ab
Matthew 19:23–30

AUGUST 19

• ST. JOHN EUDES, PRIEST •

*Going out about five o'clock, he found others standing around, and said
to them, "Why do you stand here idle all day?" They answered,
"Because no one has hired us." He said to them, "You too go
into my vineyard."*
—MATTHEW 20:6–7

Most of the time in reading this parable, I focus on how
God's freedom challenges my sense of human fairness. But
this time, I was struck by another part of the story. Why are
the workers just standing around? It's not because they aren't
interested in working but because no one has bothered to
reach out and ask them into the vineyard. Inside our bubbles,
behind our walls, and between the hedges of our vineyards
we busy ourselves. Who's waiting outside, open and ready to
meet this most generous landowner?

Ezekiel 34:1–11
Psalm 23:1–3a,3b–4,5,6
Matthew 20:1–16

AUGUST 20

• ST. BERNARD, ABBOT AND DOCTOR OF THE CHURCH •

*I will give you a new heart and place a new spirit within you, taking
from your bodies your stony hearts and giving you natural hearts. I will
put my spirit within you and make you live by my statutes, careful to
observe my decrees.*
—EZEKIEL 36:26–27

We are sometimes tempted to put various aspects of faith life
in opposition. For example, we may view love of God and
others as somehow distinct from truth and knowledge of
truth. Ezekiel won't let us get away with that here. He shares
God's vision that links intense, authentic, loving hearts with
the truth of the Lord's teaching. Today's saint, St. Bernard,
puts it another way when he writes, "What would be the
good of learning without love? It would puff up. And love
without learning? It would go astray."

Ezekiel 36:23–28
Psalm 51:12–13,14–15,18–19
Matthew 22:1–14

*Because he satisfied the longing soul
and filled the hungry soul with good things.*
—PSALM 107:9

I look outside my window, and I see a flourishing world. Birds jab at the ground, squirrels scurry and scratch, plants absorb sunlight and soak up rain, and the earth keeps turning. God provides for all of these; God satisfies. I can trust that today God, in his wisdom and love, will provide whatever it is I need to flourish as well.

Ezekiel 37:1–14
Psalm 107:2–3,4–5,6–7,8–9
Matthew 22:34–40

Call no one on earth your father; you have but one Father in heaven. Do not be called "Master"; you have but one master, the Christ.
—MATTHEW 23:9–10

What a mystery this is, this way of being human, of coming to life and knowing love. God is love, and God is the root of all love. Love is something we first learn through human beings—the mysterious, all-powerful beings we know as parents and other caregivers. What a struggle it can be, though, to journey onward and confront the limitations of that love. God worked through what they gave us, but those human beings are not God. The lessons can be painful. But on the other side is freedom. On the other side is the perfect love that never fails.

Ezekiel 43:1–7ab
Psalm 85:9ab,10,11–12,13–14
Matthew 23:1–12

Sunday

AUGUST 23

Oh, the depth of the riches and wisdom and knowledge of God! How inscrutable are his judgments and how unsearchable his ways!
—ROMANS 11:33

Through the window of our hotel room high above the streets, we could see it: The sun was setting, and it burned a gorgeous, brilliant orange, red, and yellow. I grabbed my camera and took a photo but was grievously disappointed by what I saw on the view screen: a little yellow dot—not even close. To capture, preserve, and control the richness of the Lord and all he has made is impossible. Perhaps there are moments to stop trying to put the living God and his ways in a box and focus my energies on simply living, responding, and giving thanks instead.

Isaiah 22:19–23
Psalm 138:1–2,2–3,6,8 (8bc)
Romans 11:33–36
Matthew 16:13–20

Nathanael said to him, "Can anything good come from Nazareth?"
Philip said to him, "Come and see." Jesus saw Nathanael coming toward
him and said of him, "Here is a true Israelite. There is no
duplicity in him."
—JOHN 1:46–47

Authenticity and honesty. Questions and skepticism. A simple, straightforward invitation. And here's Jesus, seeing us as we are. He offers a startling, succinct summary of Nathanael's spiritual journey. A good reminder that, by being bluntly honest and saying yes to the nudge to "come and see," we open ourselves up to the experience of meeting the Lord.

Revelation 21:9b–14
Psalm 145:10–11,12–13,17–18
John 1:45–51

AUGUST 25

• ST. LOUIS • ST. JOSEPH CALASANZ, PRIEST •

*May our Lord Jesus Christ himself and God our Father . . . encourage
your hearts and strengthen them in every good deed and word.*
—2 THESSALONIANS 2:16–17

It is so odd but endearing: I can almost always tell who my
kids have been with by how they act when they get home.
My daughter returns from time with friends speaking in the
particular cadences of her circle. A young teen boy comes
back from a visit with uncles and male cousins and his voice
is deeper than when he left (for a few minutes). They are, in
a way, implicit, unconscious witnesses to who they've
encountered. I hope I'm the same way. Specifically, I hope
that in my loving-kindness, in my openness, in my joy, in my
good deeds and words, people might be able to tell whom
I've been with and been changed by along the way.

2 Thessalonians 2:1–3a,14–17
Psalm 96:10,11–12,13
Matthew 23:23–26

AUGUST 26

*May the Lord of peace himself give you peace at all times and in every
way. The Lord be with all of you.*
—2 THESSALONIANS 3:16

We went to Mass twice on our trip to Japan. Aside from the
language, it was no different from what we experience at
home in the United States, except for one element: the sign
of peace. In Japan there's no shaking of hands or hugging at
the sign of peace. It's simply smiles and bows all around. It
might seem distant to a Westerner, but within that culture it's
an authentic way of greeting and showing respect and care.
There are all different ways we can share the Lord's peace.
What words, gestures, and thoughts will we let the Lord use
to work his peaceful ways through us today?

2 Thessalonians 3:6–10,16–18
Psalm 128:1–2,4–5
Matthew 23:27–32

Thursday
AUGUST 27
• ST. MONICA •

God is faithful, and by him you were called to fellowship with his Son,
Jesus Christ our Lord.
—1 CORINTHIANS 1:9

We may not all be mothers as St. Monica was, but we all
have had one. A mother, that is. Our relationships with our
mothers might be terrible or beautiful or somewhere in an
in-between place: bewildering, regretful, and hopeful. I'm
convinced that desire lies at the heart of our mistakes and
successes as parents, caretakers, and children. Monica desired
her son Augustine's salvation, and Augustine yearned for a
love that would not die. Around and around they went.
What is it that I desire for those I love, and where—to
whom—is it leading us?

1 Corinthians 1:1–9
Psalm 145:2–3,4–5,6–7
Matthew 24:42–51

Friday

AUGUST 28

Where is the wise one? Where is the scribe? Where is the debater of this
age? Has not God made the wisdom of the world foolish?
—1 CORINTHIANS 1:20

St. Augustine's life is an embodiment of Paul's rhetorical
questions here. He set out on that path of seeking worldly
wisdom and success. This, he discovered, was foolish, and
the notions that the world sees as foolish—God made flesh,
crucified and risen—were revealed as wisdom and truth. But
even after that, the questions didn't cease for him, and that is
both comforting and real. In his *Confessions*, Augustine
relentlessly and passionately poses questions to God. Finding
peace in the Lord doesn't mean life becomes a series of easy
answers. Questions persist because life, and God, are both so
much bigger than our understanding.

1 Corinthians 1:17–25
Psalm 33:1–2,4–5,10–11
Matthew 25:1–13

"I want you to give me at once on a platter the head of John the Baptist."
—MARK 6:25

I am not tempted by a "prosperity gospel" calling me to "name and claim" my material hopes; yet, other contemporary spiritual fads and fashions can trip me up. Feel-good book titles and programs suggest that my faith life should be exciting and awesome, enabling me to feel beautiful (*inner* beauty, right?) and empowering me to live passionately. Well, here's some passion to consider: the life of John the Baptist and his real *passion*—which actually means "suffering." His life prompts me to pause and reconsider what a passion-filled faith actually looks like.

1 Corinthians 1:26–31
Psalm 33:12–13,18–19,20–21
Mark 6:17–29

Sunday

AUGUST 30

• TWENTY-SECOND SUNDAY IN ORDINARY TIME •

Do not conform yourselves to this age but be transformed by the renewal of your mind, that you may discern what is the will of God, what is good and pleasing and perfect.
—ROMANS 12:2

Hearing Paul's words, my first instinct is to think of "this age" in cultural terms, which is certainly consistent with his meaning. But there's another way to understand this term. I live not only in a broader culture and social milieu but also in the "age" of my own life and experience, which can be a very narrow, limiting place. In prayer, that narrowness of my own "age"—my tunnel vision—is transformed by the mind of Christ, Lord of all.

Jeremiah 20:7–9
Psalm 63:2,3–4,5–6,8–9 (2b)
Romans 12:1–2
Matthew 16:21–27

AUGUST 31

[He said to them] "Again, there were many lepers in Israel during the time of Elisha the prophet; yet not one of them was cleansed, but only Naaman the Syrian." When the people in the synagogue heard this, they were all filled with fury.

—LUKE 4:27–28

Hard truths. I might well hear some hard truths today, too. They might come from Scripture, they might come in prayer, they might come from other human beings whom I encounter. How will I respond to the truth, especially when it's difficult and challenging?

1 Corinthians 2:1–5
Psalm 119:97,98,99,100,101,102
Luke 4:16–30

Tuesday

SEPTEMBER 1

And news of him spread everywhere in the surrounding region.
—LUKE 4:37

Here, the news of Jesus spread because he had taught with
authority and driven out a demon. The news continues to
spread today, and we are called to help spread it. What will
those who meet us today learn about the love of Jesus from
our words and actions? What news will we be spreading in
those encounters?

1 Corinthians 2:10b–16
Psalm 145:8–9,10–11,12–13ab,13cd–14
Luke 4:31–37

SEPTEMBER 2

At daybreak, Jesus left and went to a deserted place. The crowds went looking for him, and when they came to him, they tried to prevent him from leaving them. But he said to them, "To the other towns also I must proclaim the good news of the Kingdom of God, because for this purpose I have been sent."

—LUKE 4:42–43

It's a valuable spiritual exercise, when in a crowd of people, to look at each person and remember that he or she is on a journey, responding in some way to God's presence. Even as I focus on my own relationship with the Lord, it's good for me to remember the big purpose and picture: that enormous beautiful picture of all sorts of people, waiting, listening for the Lord Jesus to come to them.

1 Corinthians 3:1–9
Psalm 33:12–13,14–15,20–21
Luke 4:38–44

Let no one deceive himself. If anyone among you considers himself wise in this age, let him become a fool so as to become wise. For the wisdom of this world is foolishness in the eyes of God.

—1 CORINTHIANS 3:18–19

One of the most compelling aspects of Christianity is the pervasiveness of paradox and the upending of worldly expectations. St. Gregory the Great, born into wealth, took that step to become a fool for the sake of wisdom, turning from power to the monastic life. We are a people who look to teenage martyrs, beggars, and desert-dwelling hermits as our role models. We call a criminal nailed to a cross our Lord and King. Such foolishness, it seems; but without it, life doesn't even begin to make sense.

1 Corinthians 3:18–23
Psalm 24:1bc–2,3–4ab,5–6
Luke 5:1–11

It does not concern me in the least that I be judged by you or any human tribunal; I do not even pass judgment on myself; I am not conscious of anything against me, but I do not thereby stand acquitted; the one who judges me is the Lord.
—1 CORINTHIANS 4:3–4

Judgment. Expectations. Boxes, walls, and limitations. We fight them, but we also live with them and even come to accept them and take them for granted. But what if we don't have to, after all? What if there's only One to whom we're beholden, only One whose opinion of us matters? Paul's words are a powerful reminder of how true that is.

1 Corinthians 4:1–5
Psalm 37:3–4,5–6,27–28,39–40
Luke 5:33–39

SEPTEMBER 5

The LORD is near to all who call upon him.
—PSALM 145:18

There is something so freeing about formal liturgy and worship. Call it dull and dry if you like. I call it a space to which I can bring whatever feelings I'm carrying at the moment and lay them at the Lord's feet. I may be racked with grief, or I may be elated. The person next to me might be harboring doubts, and the person behind us may be wrestling with a hard decision or processing wonderful news, or simply trying to get through Mass with her toddler and her sanity intact. In the tremendous varieties of prayer types and the different Scripture readings, the Lord is near to *all*. There is space for each of us—unique and different—to pause and listen to him who beckons and readies the banquet for us.

1 Corinthians 4:6b–15
Psalm 145:17–18,19–20,21
Luke 6:1–5

SEPTEMBER 6

If your brother sins against you, go and tell him his fault between you and him alone. If he listens to you, you have won over your brother.
—MATTHEW 18:15

We all have different approaches to dealing with hurt. My tendency is to just want to let things go and to avoid confrontation. Sometimes that might be an act of mercy, a sign of forgiveness. But other times, Jesus reminds me, justice calls for more. It is, in fact, one of the spiritual works of mercy: to admonish the sinner. How difficult that can be! But in love, with Jesus present in the conversation, it is possible.

Ezekiel 33:7–9
Psalm 95:1–2,6–7,8–9
Romans 13:8–10
Matthew 18:15–20

Then Jesus said to them, "I ask you, is it lawful to do good on the sabbath rather than to do evil, to save life rather than to destroy it?"
—LUKE 6:9

Jesus knows. He reads our hearts deeply, confronting our excuses and the way we've twisted something good and made it somehow an obstacle to the good. He sees and, ever so carefully, challenges us to see too. What are we really doing here? How did our vision become so narrow? Can we be open to a richer, deeper way?

1 Corinthians 5:1–8
Psalm 5:5–6,7,12
Luke 6:6–11

SEPTEMBER 8

• THE NATIVITY OF THE BLESSED VIRGIN MARY •

Of her was born Jesus who is called the Christ.
—MATTHEW 1:16

Mary's role in Christian spirituality wasn't mandated from on high or legislated. It's the fruit of reflection on a young woman who emerges in the midst of an extraordinary, redemptive story. Try to imagine practicing and understanding Christianity without Mary. We can't. Why? Because it is one thing to proclaim the truth that "the Word became flesh and made his dwelling among us"—that God became human. It's another thing to know how to respond, as a human being, to that presence among us. Mary leads the way: a human person responding to the Lord's presence within her. How does she respond? What does she say? In her witness, I learn how to be a disciple.

Micah 5:1–4a or Romans 8:28–30
Psalm 13:6ab,6c
Matthew 1:1–16,18–23 or 1:18–23

Blessed are you who are now hungry,
for you will be satisfied.
Blessed are you who are now weeping,
for you will laugh.

—LUKE 6:21

If there's any reason I need other people in my life, it's to offer perspective. The experiences of older people help me discern what things are worth my time and energy. Around younger people, middle-aged complacency is shaken by an infusion of idealism and energy. The endurance of those who've suffered shows that one season of suffering may inform a life but does not define it. The other person I need most of all, though, is Jesus. In this Scripture I hear him proclaim another perspective that is fundamental, grounded, hopeful, and true: the rock-solid promise that beyond this earthly moment lies much, much more. Seeing this moment through his eyes with his perspective, life looks different.

1 Corinthians 7:25–31
Psalm 45:11–12,14–15,16–17
Luke 6:20–26

SEPTEMBER 10

Probe me, O God, and know my heart;
try me, and know my thoughts.
—PSALM 139:23

My mother's father died in a car accident when she was five years old. The only solid memory she had of the time was from the funeral reception: the living room carpet covered with hundreds of tiny dents made by women's sharp, narrow high heels. That's what her conscious memory retained, but who knows what deeper impact the experience of her father's death had? In daily life, how many different experiences do we have over the course of a day? Can we track the impact those experiences have on our choices and motivations? No. While it might be frightening to confront the truth of our own mystery, whatever we don't know and understand, God does.

1 Corinthians 8:1b–7,11–13
Psalm 139:1b–3,13–14ab,23–24
Luke 6:27–38

SEPTEMBER 11

*If I preach the Gospel, this is no reason for me to boast, for an obligation
has been imposed on me, and woe to me if I do not preach it!*
—1 CORINTHIANS 9:16

I live in a world filled with people who need Christ. They are
hungry for real love, the hope of eternal life, and a way out
of prisons of despair. Woe to me if I keep the Good News to
myself, if I don't open myself to letting God use me in any
small way he desires today.

1 Corinthians 9:16–19,22b–27
Psalm 84:3,4,5–6,12
Luke 6:39–42

Because the loaf of bread is one, we, though many, are one Body, for we all partake of the one loaf.
—1 CORINTHIANS 10:17

We hear a lot about the need to "create community." How does it happen? Small groups, hospitality ministries, and social activities seem to be popular approaches. Paul, though, points out something important here. We don't create Christian community, Jesus does. He's created this community—us! We are the Body of Christ, called forth in baptism, nourished with the one loaf of his body. What a profound difference it makes to look around at Mass and see people with whom we are already, right now, one in him.

1 Corinthians 10:14–22
Psalm 116:12–13,17–18
Luke 6:43–49

SEPTEMBER 13

Bless the LORD, O my soul,
and forget not all his benefits.
—PSALM 103:2

I am not particularly concerned about memory issues yet, but that doesn't stop me from being irritated by them. How in the world is it that five minutes after receiving it, I have no recollection where I shoved that ticket or receipt? It makes no sense, but I plod on, knowing now that if I'm going to remember, I have to be intentional about it. I could say something similar about my ability (or lack of it) to remember God's love and mercy. How in the world could I ever let his countless blessings slip my mind? Well, I do. And so with this, too, I must be intentional. At dawn, during the day, and at dusk, I take time and I remember.

Sirach 27:30—28:7
Psalm 103:1–2,3–4,9–10,11–12
Romans 14:7–9
Matthew 18:21–35

SEPTEMBER 14

• THE EXALTATION OF THE HOLY CROSS •

God did not send his Son into the world to condemn the world, but that the world might be saved through him.

—JOHN 3:17

One of the great challenges of the spiritual life, it seems to me, is that of staying rooted in reality. Our limited vision sometimes leads us to lurch about. We avoid hard truths one moment, but then the next moment, we're stuck in those same hard places, unable to find hope. The cross of Jesus Christ keeps us in the center. Confronted with the man on the cross every time I go into church, and, in fact, in many rooms in my own house, I can't pretend that suffering or death isn't real. But I also know what happens next, after that Friday afternoon. I know that suffering and death don't define me. I'm not condemned—I'm saved. I'm free.

Numbers 21:4b–9
Psalm 78:1bc–2,34–35,36–37,38
Philippians 2:6–11
John 3:13–17

Standing by the cross of Jesus were his mother and his mother's sister,
Mary the wife of Clopas, and Mary Magdalene.
—JOHN 19:25

When my husband died, I was a member of a parish called
Our Lady of Sorrows. Some months after his death, I was
sitting in Mass and my attention drifted to the large
stained-glass windows lining the church. Each one depicted
one of the traditional Seven Sorrows of Mary. I looked at the
window directly to my left, the burial of Jesus, and I was
jolted. This time, the scene was deeply familiar: a mourning
woman standing next to the body of a bearded man lying on
a slab. What a mystery, what a comfort, to recognize that in
these moments of sorrow, we do not grieve alone.

1 Corinthians 12:12–14,27–31a
Psalm 100:1b–2,3,4,5
John 19:25–27 or Luke 2:33–35

*If I give away everything I own, and if I hand my body over so that I
may boast but do not have love, I gain nothing.*
—1 CORINTHIANS 13:3

What is love? That attitude, that virtue, of seeing others as
God sees them, of seeking their authentic happiness and
peace in the Lord. Not as obstacles in my way, not as
instruments for me to use. Not, certainly, as "other" or
"them." What a challenge it is to really love, to let go and
abandon my will to his loving heart in everything I do.

1 Corinthians 12:31—13:13
Psalm 33:2–3,4–5,12,22
Luke 7:31–35

Thursday

SEPTEMBER 17

· ST. ROBERT BELLARMINE, BISHOP AND DOCTOR OF THE CHURCH ·

*Through it you are also being saved, if you hold fast to the word I
preached to you, unless you believed in vain.*
—1 CORINTHIANS 15:2

Some of today's choices will be minor ones: what to eat for
dinner? Others will be weightier: what advice should I give
this person in need? What about this opportunity for the
future? Paul reminds us to hold the gospel at the center of it
all, as does today's saint, Robert Bellarmine. In his book
Elevation of the Mind to God, he writes: "If you have wisdom,
may you understand that you have been created for the glory
of God and for your eternal salvation. This is your goal, this
is the centre of your soul, this is the treasure of your heart.
Therefore consider as truly good for you what leads you to
your goal, and truly evil what causes you to miss it."

1 Corinthians 15:1–11
Psalm 118:1b–2,16ab–17,28
Luke 7:36–50

> *Accompanying him were the Twelve and some women who had been cured of evil spirits and infirmities, Mary, called Magdalene, from whom seven demons had gone out.*
>
> —LUKE 8:1–2

Here she is, introduced to us for the first time: Mary, called Magdalene. It's so simple but so telling. Why had she joined the disciples? Because of what Jesus had done for her: driven out seven demons, seven being a number that symbolizes completeness. Mary had been completely possessed, her life taken over by darkness, and Jesus had freed her from it. Completely. Of course she would give her life to him in gratitude. Of course she would want to be in his presence always. Of course.

1 Corinthians 15:12–20
Psalm 17:1bcd,6–7,8b,15
Luke 8:1–3

SEPTEMBER 19

In God I trust without fear;
what can flesh do against me?
—PSALM 56:12

My then-six-year-old son said out of the blue, "It's not that I'm afraid to go to sleep without Petey. It's just that I sleep better when he's with me." It wasn't even close to bedtime, and Petey was a ratty stuffed dog. Fear, discomfort, unease—they pop up at odd times. Like my son, I might deny my fears. Like him, I might have a small anchor that keeps me grounded when they pop up unexpectedly: a thought, a prayer, a rosary in my pocket. All of these things point me toward the One who really protects me. No matter what my arms cling to in the dark, I must remember to cling ultimately to God. Lord, I give you my fears.

1 Corinthians 15:35–37,42–49
Psalm 56:10c–12,13–14
Luke 8:4–15

*I am caught between the two. I long to depart this life and be with Christ,
for that is far better. Yet that I remain in the flesh is more necessary
for your benefit.*
—PHILIPPIANS 1:23–24

I love reading St. Paul's epistles because he is real, honest,
and balanced. He's firm in his sense of his own gifts, boastful
even; yet he is also deeply humble and profoundly aware of
his weaknesses. He's combative and conciliatory. And he's
conflicted, as he expresses here. It's that honest
self-awareness that moves me. That's what happens when you
let Jesus be Lord of your life, I suppose. You know who you
are, you know who God is, and you don't get the two
confused. The fact that you're not finished here leads not to
despair but straight to hope.

Isaiah 55:6–9
Psalm 145:2–3,8–9,17–18 (18a)
Philippians 1:20c–24,27a
Matthew 20:1–16a

*But grace was given to each of us according to the measure of
Christ's gift. . . .
And he gave some as Apostles, others as prophets, others as evangelists,
others as pastors and teachers, to equip the holy ones for the work of
ministry, for building up the Body of Christ.*
—EPHESIANS 4:7,11–12

I had big ideas when I started teaching high school religion.
Well, welcome to reality. I quickly learned that while there's
this much (hold arms apart) to know, there's only this much
(hold fingers close together) time and human ability. So it is
with our role in the Body of Christ. I can sense all kinds of
needs, but I am only one person. So I move on, grateful for
whatever small gift God gives me to serve in this moment but
humbly acknowledging that I'm just one person,
one of many.

Ephesians 4:1–7,11–13
Psalm 19:2–3,4–5
Matthew 9:9–13

SEPTEMBER 22

He said to them in reply, "My mother and my brothers are those who
hear the word of God and act on it."
—LUKE 8:21

Natural and social family ties are important. But Jesus' words
here are clarifying in situations that can sometimes be fraught
with difficult dynamics. Grateful for my natural family,
mindful of my responsibilities there, I'm still called to put
Jesus, my brother, first in my life. With him, my sense of
family grows and is strengthened.

Proverbs 21:1–6,10–13
Psalm 119:1,27,30,34,35,44
Luke 8:19–21

Then they set out and went from village to village proclaiming the good news and curing diseases everywhere.
—LUKE 9:6

He's all over Italy. Pizza parlors, shops, street corners, and car windows bear the image of his bearded face. The further south you go, the more you see of him. There isn't a church in Sicily that doesn't have his statue. St. Pius of Pietrelcina, or Padre Pio, is one of the most popular saints in Italy. He's beloved as a mystic, as a doctor of souls, as the bearer of the wounds of Christ on his person, and as one present to all, especially the poor and sick. Jesus sends forth, and so the disciple goes—into every village, indeed.

Proverbs 30:5–9
Psalm 119:29,72,89,101,104,163
Luke 9:1–6

[A] thousand years in your sight
are as yesterday.
—PSALM 90:4

We spend a good amount of time with our little home microscope. We're fascinated by close-up views of everyday objects, from strands of hair to salt crystals. And then there are the living things—the protists—that we can spy on just studying the slightest bead of groundwater. One drop yields a little cosmos in which hundreds if not thousands of organisms scoot, scuttle, feed, reproduce, and die. It's a reminder of what is always going on, in every corner of life. It may be beyond our sight but never beyond the eyes of the One who created each of these lively specks. How humbling it is. How comforting, too.

Ecclesiastes 1:2–11
Psalm 90:3–4,5–6,12–13,14,17bc
Luke 9:7–9

There is an appointed time for everything,
and a time for every thing under the heavens. . . .
A time to seek, and a time to lose;
a time to keep, and a time to cast away.
—ECCLESIASTES 3:1,6

I was waiting for my kids in a crazy, six-story game complex in Osaka, Japan. Claw machines are very popular there, and any arcade you go into will have dozens of them. I watched one young girl feed several hundred-yen coins (about a dollar) into a particular machine. It was a huge stuffed hedgehog she was after. As I watched, I counted fifteen attempts—and she was still at it when we left. Persistence or folly? Sometimes, when we're in the midst of life, it's hard to tell whether it's time to keep going or time to just step away.

Ecclesiastes 3:1–11
Psalm 144:1b,2abc,3–4
Luke 9:18–22

SEPTEMBER 26

• ST. COSMAS AND ST. DAMIAN, MARTYRS •

But they did not understand this saying; its meaning was hidden from them so that they should not understand it, and they were afraid to ask him about this saying.
—LUKE 9:45

Several years ago, in working with a therapist, I offhandedly mentioned a choice my maternal grandmother had made decades before. The therapist stopped me and asked why she had done that. I didn't know, and what did it matter? "You have to ask. It matters," she said. "You have to ask your mother." Which I didn't want to do, but I did anyway. As it turned out, the answer to the mystery would provide clarity and wisdom in my own life and even in that of my daughter's later. There are many ways to seek wisdom. We listen, we seek, we observe, and sometimes we have to find courage to just ask.

Ecclesiastes 11:9—12:8
Psalm 90:3–4,5–6,12–13,14,17
Luke 9:43b–45

Sunday

SEPTEMBER 27

• TWENTY-SIXTH SUNDAY IN ORDINARY TIME •

Jesus said to the chief priests and elders of the people, "What is your opinion? A man had two sons."
—MATTHEW 21:28

Jesus invites me to believe. To believe that God exists, God is love, God forgives, and Jesus is Lord. All of this. I hear, I assent, I say the creed. But sometimes a different kind of moment emerges, the conversation shifts, the dialogue changes. Right there, in that moment, Jesus looks at me and poses a question: *What is your opinion?*

Ezekiel 18:25–28
Psalm 25:4–5,6–7,8–9 (6a)
Philippians 2:1–11 or 2:1–5
Matthew 21:28–32

SEPTEMBER 28

I call upon you, for you will answer me, O God;
incline your ear to me; hear my word.
Show your wonderous mercies,
O savior of those who flee.
—PSALM 17:6–7

Casinos are such terrible places. I've only played slots a time
or two, years ago, but had to walk through those cavernous
dungeons in places like New Orleans and Las Vegas.
Designed to keep you in place in front of that money-eating
machine, the lack of windows or clocks distorts your sense of
time. They're very concrete metaphors, it seems to me: a
metaphor for a life closed off, barricaded against the voice of
the living God. A soul fixated on the shiny task in front of
me, hoping for profit, losing track of time. Go outside. Look
up, I say to myself. Open up. Breathe.

Job 1:6–22
Psalm 17:1bcd,2–3,6–7
Luke 9:46–50

Tuesday

SEPTEMBER 29

• ST. MICHAEL, ST. GABRIEL, AND ST. RAPHAEL, ARCHANGELS •

*Jesus answered and said to him, "Do you believe because I told you that
I saw you under the fig tree? You will see greater things than this." And
he said to him, "Amen, amen, I say to you, you will see the sky opened
and the angels of God ascending and descending on the Son of Man."*

—JOHN 1:50–51

In this life on earth, there is so much more than meets the
eye. We see this truth daily (when we pay attention) in
moments of surprising grace and unexpected connections.
These small moments remind us of the greater reality to
which Jesus points us here. Life, the world, and the universe
are not flat, narrow, and one dimensional. There, just below
the surface, just beyond my senses are angels, the
communion of saints, the eternal height, depth, and breadth
of life with the eternal God.

Daniel 7:9–10,13–14 or Revelation 12:7–12a
Psalm 138:1–2ab,2cde–3,4–5
John 1:47–51

No one who sets a hand to the plow and looks to what was left behind is fit for the Kingdom of God.
—LUKE 9:62

In visiting museums and historic churches when my children were young, we played a saints guessing game. Saints have certain "attributes"—objects associated with them in visual art. Who is the man with the short beard and the rooster? (Peter) Who's the woman dressed in red, with the jar? (Mary Magdalene) Saint Jerome was easy: he's the wizened man in the desert or in a study, surrounded by books and accompanied by a lion. It's an entertaining game, but in contemplating these symbolic attributes, I'm challenged to dig deeper. What attributes and characteristics of a disciple fit for the kingdom is the world seeing in me? I pray they will see mercy, agape love, and total openness to the Lord's call.

Job 9:1–12,14–16
Psalm 88:10bc–11,12–13,14–15
Luke 9:57–62

Thursday

OCTOBER 1

*Go on your way; behold, I am sending you like lambs among wolves.
Carry no money bag, no sack, no sandals; and greet no one
along the way.*
—LUKE 10:3–4

One of the best-selling spiritual books in history is
St. Thérèse's *Story of a Soul*. But here's the thing: she didn't
want to write it. It was only under obedience that she left the
record of her spiritual journey. I think about that a lot in our
era of self-promotion and platforms and evangelization
efforts that are dependent on personalities and marketing. I
listen to Jesus here, I consider the impact of St. Thérèse,
quietly, anonymously living her Little Way; my assumptions
are challenged, my vision is refocused to center on each
moment, each opportunity to love in the present, with no
self-serving agenda except that: to love.

Job 19:21–27
Psalm 27:7–8a,8b–9abc,13–14
Luke 10:1–12

"Amen, I say to you, unless you turn and become like children, you will not enter the Kingdom of heaven. Whoever humbles himself like this child is the greatest in the Kingdom of heaven."
—MATTHEW 18:3–4

Jesus lived in a culture that treated children as creatures lacking the faculties that defined a full human being. To present a *child*—who could be exploited and killed when inconvenient—as a model for the spiritual life? Absurd. Countercultural. A radical, reality-shifting stance. It is easy for me to shake my head at their narrowness in the distant past, but Jesus still lives, the gospel is still preached, and it is preached to me. Jesus challenges my modern assumptions too. How do I respond? Defensively, rationalizing because I know better? Or can I listen . . . like a child?

Job 38:1,12–21; 40:3–5
Psalm 139:1–3,7–8,9–10,13–14ab
Matthew 18:1–5,10

I had heard of you by word of mouth,
but now my eye has seen you.
—JOB 42:5

I am not sure how the saying "the patience of Job" came
about, because when you dive into the story, Job is not
actually very patient. After suffering paralyzing personal
losses, his friends advise him to just take it and move on. But
Job won't. He argues, seethes, and questions. And in the end,
what happens? Job encounters God. True, what God says to
him is tough, basically asking "Who are you to question my
ways?" But we can take away much from this complex story.
We see not only the truth of the mystery of God's ways but
also the fruit of Job's deep questioning and honest struggle:
an encounter with the presence of God.

Job 42:1–3,5–6,12–17
Psalm 119:66,71,75,91,125,130
Luke 10:17–24

Sunday

OCTOBER 4

• TWENTY-SEVENTH SUNDAY IN ORDINARY TIME •

Have no anxiety at all, but in everything, by prayer and petition, with
thanksgiving, make your requests known to God. Then the peace of God
that surpasses all understanding will guard your hearts and minds
in Christ Jesus.
—PHILIPPIANS 4:6–7

In the weeks after my husband died suddenly at the age of
fifty, I couldn't imagine ever being at peace again. But over
ten years later, here we are, bearing scars but certainly (I
think) mostly whole. I'm convinced that prayer played a part.
Hundreds of people prayed for us and for his soul. That's
why, when people ask even in passing, "Pray for me," I try to
set aside a second of my life and do just that, praying that
God's peace, so mysterious yet so close at hand,
will keep them.

Isaiah 5:1–7
Psalm 80:9,12,13–14,15–16,19–20
Philippians 4:6–9
Matthew 21:33–43

He approached the victim, poured oil and wine over his wounds and bandaged them. Then he lifted him up on his own animal, took him to an inn and cared for him. The next day he took out two silver coins and gave them to the innkeeper with the instruction, "Take care of him."
—LUKE 10:34–35

Some ancient spiritual writers suggested that we think of this Samaritan—this outcast—as Jesus himself. Jesus is the one who saves us, those beaten by sin and left for dead. He rescues us and leaves us in the care of the innkeeper, the church. So we are both the wounded and those given the gift and responsibility to continue sharing the healing power of the One who found us on his way to Jerusalem.

Galatians 1:6–12
Psalm 111:1b–2,7–8,9,10c
Luke 10:25–37

Tuesday

OCTOBER 6

• ST. BRUNO, PRIEST • BLESSED MARIE ROSE DUROCHER, VIRGIN •

The Lord said to her in reply, "Martha, Martha, you are anxious and
worried about many things."
—LUKE 10:41

How many times have I considered time to read Scripture,
pray the rosary, or just quietly be in God's presence and said,
"Not now. Later. Too much to do"? Many. How many times
have I readied myself for Mass and fought off feelings of
reluctance? Too often. And how many times, having plunged
through the reluctance and resisted the temptation to busy
myself elsewhere, have I ever regretted that time spent with
the Lord? Never.

Galatians 1:13–24
Psalm 139:1b–3,13–14ab,14c–15
Luke 10:38–42

OCTOBER 7

• OUR LADY OF THE ROSARY •

He said to them, "When you pray, say:
Father, hallowed be your name,
your Kingdom come.
Give us each day our daily bread
and forgive us our sins."
—LUKE 11:2–4

A previous retreatant had left her notes in the Bible of my room in the retreat center. The notes were, I'd guess, the fruit of prayer time. The theme of the list was fear and was summed up in the words, underlined twice, *Pray more. Fear less.* No matter what our specific needs, Jesus teaches us in this moment how to begin and orient ourselves: honor God first, acknowledge his priority in our lives, then . . . just present our needs to him, confidently—without fear.

Galatians 2:1–2,7–14
Psalm 117:1bc,2
Luke 11:1–4

I tell you, ask and you will receive; seek and you will find; knock and the door will be opened to you.
—LUKE 11:10

A woman at the convenience-store counter was speaking earnestly to the cashier. She had a pen and a Bible, open to the endpapers filled with handwritten names. "And this is Ellen down at the pharmacy, and Joe, too. I've got Mark from the Piggly Wiggly." She added, "I'll put your name here." Those endpapers in her Bible were filled, I realized, with the names of people she prayed for. If I'd been a braver woman, I'd have asked her to add my name to her list, and asked for hers. As it is, I'll try to let that generous spirit inform my own daily encounters with others, all in need of prayer.

Galatians 3:1–5
Luke 1:69–70,71–72,73–75
Luke 11:5–13

Friday

OCTOBER 9

Majesty and glory are his work,
and his justice endures forever.
—PSALM 111:3

On the outskirts of Paris, far from the usual tourist paths, stands one of the more important churches in Europe. It is the Cathedral of Saint-Denis, the third-century bishop of Paris whose feast is celebrated today. The cathedral is famous not only for its Gothic architecture but also for its vast collection of funeral statuary. Recumbent stone monarchs fill much of the space, most of them dressed in appropriate royal robes, with a few fascinating exceptions. Louis XII and Anne of Brittany's tomb is topped by images of them kneeling in prayer, fully dressed; then, in a space below, we see them again, lying as in death, completely nude. It is a startling, sobering sight, a reminder that human glory doesn't last. Only God's glory and majesty will last forever.

Galatians 3:7–14
Psalm 111:1b–2,3–4,5–6
Luke 11:15–26

OCTOBER 10

There is neither Jew nor Greek, there is neither slave nor free person, there is not male and female; for you are all one in Christ Jesus.
—GALATIANS 3:28

When I worked as a cashier back in college, customers were an irritant. Now, as a customer, how often do I fight annoyance at a cashier? As a teacher, I wanted to blame parents for education's ills. As a parent of students, I rant about the schools. In other words, division in this world is real, and I can't deny my own contribution to it. But it doesn't have to be that way. Paul reminds me that in my baptism, I take on another way of seeing those around me: as brothers and sisters, one in him.

Galatians 3:22–29
Psalm 105:2–3,4–5,6–7
Luke 11:27–28

Sunday

OCTOBER 11

• TWENTY-EIGHTH SUNDAY IN ORDINARY TIME •

*I know how to live in humble circumstances; I know also how
to live with abundance.*
—PHILIPPIANS 4:12

When we think about living in humble circumstances,
St. Francis of Assisi comes to mind. After all, he is *Il Poverello*,
"The Poor One." When you actually read St. Francis's
writings, it's interesting to note that he emphasizes poverty
for his brothers, but he doesn't issue a general call for all
people to voluntarily embrace material poverty. Francis
emphasizes more the radical nature of the poverty of Christ:
the total gift of self and an emptying of the will for the sake
of the Father. This doesn't give us an excuse or a
rationalization to cling to our stuff but, rather, the simple
recognition that to embrace poverty means, above all, to
give—not just what you have but who you are.

Isaiah 25:6–10a
Psalm 23:1–3a,3b–4,5,6 (6cd)
Philippians 4:12–14,19–20
Matthew 22:1–14 or 22:1–10

OCTOBER 12

For freedom Christ set us free; so stand firm and do not submit again to the yoke of slavery.
—GALATIANS 5:1

When I taught high school theology, I don't know if there was a theme I was more passionate about than freedom in Christ. When I looked out at my students, I would see and hear so much sadness related to the feeling that they were being judged: by peers, family members, and just the world in general. How many times did I say it—that the only one we are bound to is Christ, and there, in the communion, real freedom awaits. Listen to him, love him, and please him. Start there, claim your freedom, and find peace.

Galatians 4:22–24,26–27,31—5:1
Psalm 113:1b–2,3–4,5a,6–7
Luke 11:29–32

The Pharisee was amazed to see that he did not observe the prescribed washing before the meal. The Lord said to him, "Oh you Pharisees! Although you cleanse the outside of the cup and the dish, inside you are filled with plunder and evil."

—LUKE 11:38–39

I made it to Mass. During the week! I didn't eat meat last Friday. Good for me. But wait. How did I treat my children that day? What was in my heart when I saw my neighbor? What was my response to a plea for help? Did my spiritual practices work to open me to grace and giving, or did they do no more than polish the outside?

OCTOBER 14

• ST. CALLISTUS I, POPE AND MARTYR •

Now those who belong to Christ [Jesus] have crucified their flesh with its passions and desires. If we live in the Spirit, let us also follow the Spirit.
—GALATIANS 5:24–25

Years ago, for twenty-four hours each month, I would plunge into despair. It was suggested to me that tracking my cycle might reveal a physiological reason for this swing. I was resistant. Don't tell me that my existential angst is "only" PMS! Well, I finally took that advice, and surprise, surprise—it tracked. Megadoses of B vitamins went a long way in diminishing the power that hormonal surge (or dip) had over me. The fact of body chemistry gives an interesting twist to Paul's call to crucify our flesh. All the more reason, I think, to tie my sense of self to the rock of God's love for me, not what my flawed and weak body tells me.

Galatians 5:18–25
Psalm 1:1–2,3,4,6
Luke 11:42–46

Blessed be the God and Father of our Lord Jesus Christ, who has blessed
us in Christ with every spiritual blessing in the heavens.
—EPHESIANS 1:3

Paul, tireless and active, helped others in every corner of the known world meet Christ. Teresa of Jesus, active in her own way, focused on reforming religious life, stripping it of distractions, also enabling others to meet Christ in the quiet of their simple spaces. Paul inspires my restless spirit; Teresa calms me down and centers me. In *The Way of Perfection*, she reminds us of a vital truth about where those blessings Paul speaks of can be found: "[W]e need no wings to go in search of Him but have only to find a place where we can be alone and look upon Him present within us."

Ephesians 1:1–10
Psalm 98:1,2–3ab,3cd–4,5–6
Luke 11:47–54

• ST. HEDWIG, RELIGIOUS • ST. MARGARET MARY ALACOQUE, VIRGIN •

There is nothing concealed that will not be revealed, nor secret that will not be known.
—LUKE 12:2

An errant stone from a weed eater hit the patio door. The glass immediately cracked, but since it was safety glass, it didn't shatter. In the weeks it took to get a replacement, those cracks took over the door like a giant spider web until one day, a huge section of glass just crumbled. It was finally fixed, but even weeks later, we kept finding little nuggets of glass, glinting in the light on the living room floor. In Jesus, my sins are forgiven. The impact of those sins can remain, though, can't they? The habits, the wounds—they keep turning up. It's only when they're revealed under the light Jesus brings that I can begin to sweep them away for good.

Ephesians 1:11–14
Psalm 33:1–2,4–5,12–13
Luke 12:1–7

Saturday

OCTOBER 17

• ST. IGNATIUS OF ANTIOCH, BISHOP AND MARTYR •

Brothers and sisters: Hearing of your faith in the Lord Jesus and of your love for the holy ones, I do not cease giving thanks for you, remembering you in my prayers.
—EPHESIANS 1:15–16

Today is the memorial of St. Ignatius of Antioch, who was marched across Asia Minor to be executed in Rome. He wrote letters along the way, as did, of course, Paul. Saint Ignatius's letters, like Paul's here to the Ephesians, are courageous and joyful, rooted in trust in Jesus' promise despite what he knew lay ahead. I communicate all day long in formal and informal ways, off-the-cuff or planned, to those I'm close to and to strangers. In all of those varied circumstances—what's my message going to be?

Ephesians 1:15–23
Psalm 8:2–3ab,4–5,6–7
Luke 12:8–12

Sunday
OCTOBER 18

• TWENTY-NINTH SUNDAY IN ORDINARY TIME •

*Paul, Silvanus, and Timothy to the church of the Thessalonians in God
the Father and the Lord Jesus Christ: grace to you and peace.*
—1 THESSALONIANS 1:1

At this time of year, this happens where I live: People who
are strangers to each other say as a greeting, "Roll, Tide!" At
the grocery checkout line or the gas station or the coffee
shop, class, ethnic, and gender divisions effortlessly
disappear. College football spirit ties everyone together. But
the ties that bind us to other believers go so much deeper. In
Christ, God has joined us together as his church, where we
can greet one another with grace and peace. We are in
communion with all the baptized, called to know each other
not by the colors we wear but by our love.

Isaiah 45:1,4–6
Psalm 96:1,3,4–5,7–8,9–10 (7b)
1 Thessalonians 1:1–5b
Matthew 22:15–21

⇒ 323 ⇐

OCTOBER 19

• ST. JOHN DE BRÉBEUF AND ST. ISAAC JOGUES, PRIESTS, AND
COMPANIONS, MARTYRS •

*For we are his handiwork, created in Christ Jesus for good works that
God has prepared in advance, that we should live in them.*
—EPHESIANS 2:10

The seventeenth-century French Jesuit St. John de Brébeuf
wrote guidelines for other missionaries coming to the New
World. The instructions are striking because they are infused
with a deep sense of the humanity and dignity of the
Canadian indigenous peoples. In the book *Jesuit Relations*, he
is quoted as saying: "You must have a sincere affection for the
Huron—looking upon them as ransomed by the blood of the
Son of God, and as our brethren with whom we are to pass
the rest of our lives." My life is certainly different from his,
but the challenge is the same: to view (and treat) those
among whom I walk every day as brothers and
sisters—God's handiwork.

Ephesians 2:1–10
Psalm 100:1b–2,3,4ab,4c–5
Luke 12:13–21

Tuesday

OCTOBER 20

• ST. PAUL OF THE CROSS, PRIEST •

Near indeed is his salvation to those who fear him,
glory dwelling in our land.
—PSALM 85:10

It might be one of the most difficult aspects of faith: trusting that the Lord is indeed near. We encounter countless obstacles to trusting in his presence, don't we? Some of those are of our own making; others stand in our way as manifestations of a sinful, broken world. What a revelation, then, to realize that the distance we feel isn't what God wants. He is indeed near, waiting.

Ephesians 2:12–22
Psalm 85:9ab–10,11–12,13–14
Luke 12:35–38

OCTOBER 21

Much will be required of the person entrusted with much, and still more will be demanded of the person entrusted with more.
—LUKE 12:48

If I'd been born a couple of centuries ago, there's no doubt I would have been considered blind. I'm so nearsighted that without my contacts or glasses, everything beyond about six inches from my eyes is a blur. If I had to live in that fog every day with no respite, unable to see the details in the landscape or even what's across the room, it would be unimaginable. I'm so grateful for how human beings have used the gifts God gave them to help others flourish. It gives me pause, as well. Such an advantage I have over the me that would have lived two hundred years ago. What am I doing with that gift of greater sight—and all the rest of my gifts—right here, today?

Ephesians 3:2–12
Isaiah 12:2–3,4bcd,5–6
Luke 12:39–48

Thursday

OCTOBER 22

From now on a household of five will be divided, three against two and two against three; a father will be divided against his son and a son against his father, a mother against her daughter and a daughter against her mother, a mother-in-law against her daughter-in-law and a daughter-in-law against her mother-in-law.

—LUKE 12:52–53

The cost may be high and deeply countercultural, but no matter what, Jesus calls, and to him, I listen.

Ephesians 3:14–21
Psalm 33:1–2,4–5,11–12,18–19
Luke 12:49–53

Friday

OCTOBER 23

• ST. JOHN OF CAPISTRANO, PRIEST •

The LORD's are the earth and its fullness;
the world and those who dwell in it.
—PSALM 24:1

My son's jazz teacher grew up in a Communist country. In an interview, he said something that made me laugh because of its simplicity and directness. It also struck me as coming from a deeply spiritual perspective. The interviewer commented on the musician's very conceptual approach to his music. My son's teacher agreed, saying that growing up in a country like his at that time, a person always had to think about "the big picture, or else you'd get depressed." How true, no matter where you live. Keeping our eyes on those big-picture truths—God is our Creator and we are his—is the bedrock of spiritual health and wholeness.

Ephesians 4:1–6
Psalm 24:1–2,3–4ab,5–6
Luke 12:54–59

Saturday

OCTOBER 24

• ST. ANTHONY MARY CLARET, BISHOP •

Let us go rejoicing to the house of the Lord.
—*See* PSALM 122:1

On the vigil of a feast, we wandered through the center of Puebla, Mexico. Painted, tiled, Baroque church towers stood every few blocks, and so every few blocks we stepped into a celebration. We would go to Mass the next morning, but this evening, I simply wanted to hear the music, see the church decor, and get a sense of how people were worshipping. But wasn't it awkward and impolite to just be looking in during Mass? Didn't heads turn? Not at all. For these are not private fortresses with a tightly managed flow. No, they are traditionally constructed churches set on busy streets, doors flung wide open during Mass, welcoming without judgment or a second glance all who might be drawn, for whatever reason, to the life within God's house.

Ephesians 4:7–16
Psalm 122:1–2,3–4ab,4cd–5
Luke 13:1–9

He said to him, "You shall love the Lord, your God, with all your heart, with all your soul, and with all your mind. This is the greatest and the first commandment."
—MATTHEW 22:37–38

We belong to a local Jewish recreation center, mostly for the fantastic pool. A side effect of swimming time is education. In talking about the Jewish holidays on which the center is closed, about the kosher menu at the snack bar, about the fact that the vending machines are shut off on the Sabbath, my kids have learned a lot. Most striking is the fact that there's a mezuzah at every door. This is a small container that holds a scroll of the *Shema*—the prayer that contains, in part, the Scripture Jesus quotes here. Every step I take, every passage, I'm reminded: above all, love him.

Exodus 22:20–26
Psalm 18:2–3,3–4,47,51
1 Thessalonians 1:5c–10
Matthew 22:34–40

OCTOBER 26

*Let no one deceive you with empty arguments, for because of these things
the wrath of God is coming upon the disobedient. So do not be
associated with them.*
—EPHESIANS 5:6–7

Paul warns us away from associating with certain unbelievers.
But aren't we supposed to engage with the world? Isn't God
in all things? Well, yes. But as with everything else,
discernment is important and has to be used continuously, I
think. There are times in which it's good for me to engage
with people, places, things, and ideas that stand counter to
the gospel if I'm strong and supported and really discern
that's where God wants me to be at that moment. But there
are other times in which it's better, for my own sake, to close
the door, center my spirit on the Lord, and entrust the paths
on which others journey to him.

Ephesians 4:32—5:8
Psalm 1:1–2,3,4,6
Luke 13:10–17

OCTOBER 27

*Again he said, "To what shall I compare the Kingdom of God? It is like
yeast that a woman took and mixed in with three measures of wheat flour
until the whole batch of dough was leavened."*
—LUKE 13:20–21

Yeast, of course, is alive. It's alive like the mustard seed Jesus
had just spoken of. It's alive, just waiting for the proper
conditions to grow and flourish. This is a wonderful picture
of God's kingdom and the life of faith: living, growing,
transforming. And like that seed that grows into a
shelter-giving bush, like that yeast that creates nourishing
food—it gives life.

Ephesians 5:21–33
Psalm 128:1–2,3,4–5
Luke 13:18–21

Brothers and sisters: You are no longer strangers and sojourners, but you are fellow citizens with the holy ones and members of the household of God.
—EPHESIANS 2:19

Paul is writing to Gentiles here. Once alienated from the one true God, the God of Israel, now they are family in Christ. All barriers have been broken, and they are home. Recall the resistance Paul met to this great movement of the Spirit. Sometimes, even as baptized church members, we don't feel "at home" in a particular community, and we seek a deeper sense of welcome. When we feel like outsiders, it's good to remember Paul's words and the simple truth: no matter how other human beings or circumstances make us feel, every church community is our home. We belong there because we belong to him.

Ephesians 2:19–22
Psalm 19:2–3,4–5
Luke 6:12–16

OCTOBER 29

"Jerusalem, Jerusalem, you who kill the prophets and stone those sent to you, how many times I yearned to gather your children together as a hen gathers her brood under her wings, but you were unwilling!"

—LUKE 13:34

Jesus invites, Jesus offers mercy, and Jesus seeks to gather us in love. Are we willing to be open, willing to be gathered with the other mercy seekers, the rest of the broken, under his wings? Or are we still resisting, still standing apart, believing that we don't need the healing Jesus offers?

Ephesians 6:10–20
Psalm 144:1b,2,9–10
Luke 13:31–35

[T]his is my prayer: that your love may increase ever more and more in knowledge and every kind of perception, to discern what is of value, so that you may be pure and blameless for the day of Christ.
—PHILIPPIANS 1:9–10

We pray for people all the time. We pray for their health. We pray for their happiness and peace of mind. We pray for an end to their suffering, or at least to find peace in that suffering. Today, let's do something different. Let's allow Paul's prayer for the Philippians to settle in our hearts. Let it bring to mind all those for whom we are praying for deeper faith and closeness to Christ.

Philippians 1:1–11
Psalm 111:1–2,3–4,5–6
Luke 14:1–6

OCTOBER 31

"For everyone who exalts himself will be humbled, but the one who humbles himself will be exalted."
—LUKE 14:11

On this night called Halloween or All Hallows' Eve, what are we doing but living out the call of Jesus in a very particular way? Think about it. Strangers come to our doors, strangers who might even be trying to frighten us. And what do we do? We welcome them! We share some of what we have. Yes, it's a game; yes, it's a party of sorts; and no, no one really needs candy. But perhaps it's just one more small way to practice Jesus' way of welcoming, openness, and humility.

Philippians 1:18b–26
Psalm 42:2,3,5cdef
Luke 14:1,7–11

After this I had a vision of a great multitude, which no one could count,
from every nation, race, people, and tongue.
—REVELATION 7:9

Sometimes when I hear Jesus' words and see the life he lived,
the call to follow him seems impossible. Beyond what any
human being could do. The great multitude of saints—young
and elderly, powerful and homeless, energetic and retiring,
from every corner of the globe—show me that it's not.

Revelation 7:2–4,9–14
Psalm 24:1bc–2,3–4ab,5–6
1 John 3:1–3
Matthew 5:1–12a

• THE COMMEMORATION OF ALL THE FAITHFUL DEPARTED
(ALL SOULS' DAY) •

For I am convinced that neither death, nor life, nor angels, nor principalities, nor present things, nor future things, nor powers, nor height, nor depth, nor any other creature will be able to separate us from the love of God in Christ Jesus our Lord.
—ROMANS 8:38–39

At the funeral of a retired bishop, the homilist reminded us that the deceased had frequently said, "When I die, please pray for me and don't stop." Oddly enough, I remember my late husband saying the exact same thing. Little did either of us know that a few months later I would have a reason to remember his words. I have prayed for him. Not only for him, but for all the faithful departed, the numbers of whom grow by the year as I get older. And so I pray, confident that in the power of Christ nothing can separate all of us from life eternal.

Wisdom 3:1–9
Romans 5:5–11 or 8:31b–35,37–39
John 6:37–40
Other readings may be selected.

"A man gave a great dinner to which he invited many. When the time for the dinner came, he dispatched his servant to say to those invited, 'Come, everything is now ready.' But one by one, they all began to excuse themselves."

—LUKE 14:16–18

The grindingly slow process of filmmaking is interesting, and we like to go watch when a movie production comes to town. Right now it's an action movie with streets blocked off, smashed and smoking cars, and lots of running and yelling. They do it again and again until it seems right, and then they film it, with the certainty that later editing can fix what's lacking. We don't have that option in real life, do we? Certainly, the Lord forgives our "bad takes"—our sins and errors. But now, in this moment, whether we are ready or not, he is inviting us to dine with him. No second takes, no replays, no excuses.

Philippians 2:5–11
Psalm 22:26b–27,28–30ab,30e,31–32
Luke 14:15–24

"Whoever does not carry his own cross and come after me cannot be my disciple."
—LUKE 14:27

St. Charles Borromeo was a reforming bishop of sixteenth-century Milan. Where did he begin his reforms? With himself. The Borromeos were a very wealthy family, and Carlos could easily have followed the pampered path of a typical aristocratic cleric, but he didn't. In 2010, in a message marking the four-hundredth anniversary of St. Borromeo's canonization, Pope Emeritus Benedict XVI observed, "Charles Borromeo neither limited himself to deploring or condemning nor merely to hoping that others would change, but rather set about reforming his own life which, after he had abandoned wealth and ease, he filled with prayer, penance and loving dedication to his people." It's a lot easier to tell others how they need to change than to hear Christ's call and let my own life be radically changed by the cross.

Philippians 2:12–18
Psalm 27:1,4,13–14
Luke 14:25–33

NOVEMBER 5

"*And when she does find it, she calls together her friends and neighbors and says to them, 'Rejoice with me because I have found the coin that I lost.' In just the same way, I tell you, there will be rejoicing among the angels of God over one sinner who repents.*"

—LUKE 15:9–10

Sin distances us from God. Perhaps that's part of the paradigm of temptation. The darkness seeks to draw us in, and stuck in the corner like a lost coin, the dust disfigures us and darkens what once glimmered with hope. But even there—especially there—we are still sought after and hoped for. He's searching for us; he wants us back; and when we enter his light again—there is rejoicing.

Philippians 3:3–8a
Psalm 105:2–3,4–5,6–7
Luke 15:1–10

NOVEMBER 6

I rejoiced because they said to me,
"We will go up to the house of the LORD."
—PSALM 122:1

My son developed a deep interest in ancient Mayan culture.
Spring break rolled around, so we decided to engage that
interest and travel to the Yucatan. I'll never forget the first
time he stood in the ancient ball court in the ruins of
Chichen Itza. With a wondrous grin he chortled, "I can't
believe I'm really here!" So it is when we arrive at a new,
anticipated, exciting place. And so it is for most of us when
we return home as well. It's all cause for joy: the new and the
familiar, the exciting and the safe. I'm thinking that in our
ultimate home with the Lord, we'll find both, ever new and
ever secure—all at once, all at the same time, for eternity.

Philippians 3:17—4:1
Psalm 122:1–2,3–4ab,4cd–5
Luke 16:1–8

*In every circumstance and in all things . . . I have the strength for
everything through him who empowers me.*
—PHILIPPIANS 4:13

A friend was the musical director of a local college
production. Afterward, I complimented him on his great
work with the students, but, I ventured to say, I really didn't
like the play itself. He immediately agreed: "Oh, that show is
just no good." That prompted a good conversation with my
puzzled son, who was listening. Not everything we engage
with is our ideal situation. Sometimes we are called to change
that, sometimes not. Nonetheless, God is still present,
inviting us to let him work through our efforts in fruitful,
loving ways.

Philippians 4:10–19
Psalm 112:1b–2,5–6,8a,9
Luke 16:9–15

NOVEMBER 8

• THIRTY-SECOND SUNDAY IN ORDINARY TIME •

Therefore, stay awake, for you know neither the day nor the hour.
—MATTHEW 25:13

When Italians answer the phone, they don't say hello in Italian. Rather, the traditional Italian phone greeting is *Pronto!*—which translates as "Ready!" One theory I've read is that the greeting originated in the era of switchboards, when you'd tell the operator you were ready to be connected. I don't know the truth of that, but I love the practice. It wouldn't be a bad practice to internalize this idea for life in general. In every moment the Lord invites me to watch for him, to be ready, to dig deeper and draw closer. Instead of looking back, instead of saying, "Well, but I . . ."—how about today I say *Pronto!*

Wisdom 6:12–16
Psalm 63:2,3–4,5–6,7–8 (2b)
1 Thessalonians 4:13–18 or 4:13–14
Matthew 25:1–13

You are God's building. According to the grace of God given to me, like a wise master builder I laid a foundation, and another is building upon it. But each one must be careful how he builds upon it, for no one can lay a foundation other than the one that is there, namely,
Jesus Christ.

—1 CORINTHIANS 3:9c–11

Once again we encounter Paul's realism and wisdom. He is honest about the interplay between human and divine action. We act, we move, we choose, we bring our uniqueness to the moment as we plunge into the mission field of life. But we do so always with Christ as the foundation, our center and our guide.

Ezekiel 47:1–2,8–9,12
Psalm 46:2–3,5–6,8–9
1 Corinthians 3:9c–11,16–17
John 2:13–22

NOVEMBER 10

• ST. LEO THE GREAT, POPE AND DOCTOR OF THE CHURCH •

Trust in the LORD and do good.
—PSALM 37:3

It's not uncommon to struggle as we discern how to develop and share our gifts. We might be tempted to wait for that perfect moment, when all the obstacles are cleared away. Surely that's what it takes to use our gifts well? Maybe not, as I learned a few years ago when I read the letters of Michelangelo. The great artist was beset by problems, including self-doubt, frustration, family pressures, and financial distractions. He writes in one letter to Luigi del Riccio: "How much better it would have been if in my early days I had been set to make sulfur matches, for then I should not have all this anxiety!" Perhaps, then, the "perfect moment" for doing the good the Lord has called us to is the present moment, messy and real.

Titus 2:1–8,11–14
Psalm 37:3–4,18,23,27,29
Luke 17:7–10

*And one of them, realizing he had been healed, returned, glorifying God
in a loud voice; and he fell at the feet of Jesus and thanked him.*
—LUKE 17:15–16

Lining the walls of the museum at the shrine to Our Lady of
Guadalupe in Mexico was something I had never seen before:
ex-voto paintings. These were small, primitive, hand-painted
scenes depicting how the prayers of the sick, the injured, and
the imprisoned had been answered by Our Lady. They were
at once charming, raw, honest, and so expressive of deep
gratitude. I couldn't help but pause, examine my own life,
remember answered prayers and the healing grace of God,
and then join my grateful prayer to the scores echoing
around me.

Titus 3:1–7
Psalm 23:1b–3a,3bc–4,5,6
Luke 17:11–19

Perhaps this is why he was away from you for a while, that you might have him back forever, no longer as a slave but more than a slave, a brother, beloved especially to me, but even more so to you, as a man and in the Lord.

—PHILEMON 15–16

The story of Paul, Onesimus, and Philemon is interesting and challenging. Paul met the escaped slave Onesimus in prison and led him to faith in Christ. When Onesimus was released from prison, Paul sent this letter with him to his master, Philemon. He doesn't argue against slavery, but he does introduce a radical element in an accepted reality: "You know your slave? Well, that man is now your brother." We may walk in a fallen world, but wherever we walk, whatever the brokenness, we can still bring Christ there.

Philemon 7–20
Psalm 146:7,8–9a,9bc–10
Luke 17:20–25

NOVEMBER 13

• ST. FRANCES XAVIER CABRINI, VIRGIN •

With all my heart I seek you;
Let me not stray from your commands.
—PSALM 119:10

Whenever I feel as if it's all too much, that this discipleship business is beyond me and perhaps beyond all normal human beings, I consider the life of St. Frances Cabrini. Making a map of her travels founding hospitals, schools, and orphanages would mean tracing a path from Italy across the Atlantic, all around the United States, from New York to Colorado to New Orleans, then into South America, and then back to Chicago, where she died. I can't follow in her footsteps exactly, but if I can give over just a bit more of my heart to the Lord and his children, then in a way, I am.

2 John 4–9
Psalm 119:1,2,10,11,17,18
Luke 17:26–37

NOVEMBER 14

Jesus told his disciples a parable about the necessity for them to pray always without becoming weary.
—LUKE 18:1

"Necessity." I noticed that word particularly in this reading. Jesus doesn't give encouragement or simply offer an argument for praying without ceasing. He tells the disciples a story—always the most powerful way of teaching—to help them see that it's necessary to keep praying, even when we wonder what the point is. If we want to understand this better, it helps to imagine the opposite. What if we stopped praying? What would be the shape and direction of our lives without prayer? Well, Jesus is right again. It *is* necessary.

3 John 5–8
Psalm 112:1–2,3–4,5–6
Luke 18:1–8

⇒ 350 ⇐

For to everyone who has, more will be given and he will grow rich.
—MATTHEW 25:29

My neighbor has a vintage red and white RV trailer parked in her driveway, a few feet from my kitchen window. We have lived here for over six years, and it's never been moved; no one's ever used it or even cracked a door open on it. The years pass, colors fade, dirt collects, and there it sits. I try not to be "that neighbor," but yes, I get irritated. Why does she have it sitting there if she's not going to use it? But then I listen to what I'm saying, and I accept that perhaps I'd be better off (as usual) turning that question around. What has the Lord given me? What am I doing with it? Is it just sitting there, deep within, gathering dust?

Proverbs 31:10–13,19–20,30–31
Psalm 128:1–2,3,4–5
1 Thessalonians 5:1–6
Matthew 25:14–30 or 25:14–15,19–21

*The people walking in front rebuked him, telling him to be silent, but he
kept calling out all the more, "Son of David, have pity on me!" Then
Jesus stopped and ordered that he be brought to him; and when he came
near, Jesus asked him, "What do you want me to do for you?" He
replied, "Lord, please let me see."*

—LUKE 18:39–41

I love so much about this narrative. The very believable
scenario of passersby telling the blind man to be quiet and
keep his problems to himself. The man's persistence, and his
trust in who Jesus is and his confidence in what he can do.
Most of all, I am always struck by Jesus' question, and then
the man's simple direct response. We make many things
(including the life of faith) so very complicated. Do they
have to be?

Revelation 1:1–4; 2:1–5
Psalm 1:1–2,3,4,6
Luke 18:35–43

If someone who has worldly means sees a brother in need and refuses him compassion, how can the love of God remain in him?
—1 JOHN 3:17

Thanksgiving is not until next week, but we're probably already making plans for celebrating our gratitude. Many of us will gather with those we know best within familiar walls. But is there another way? Every Thanksgiving a restaurant down the road from me offers a free meal. If you can pay, fine, and any money they collect goes to a shelter. If you're unable to pay, no problem. You're welcome to the feast no matter what. St. Elizabeth of Hungary, noble born, might easily have focused her days on preserving her way of life behind protective walls and closed doors. But she heard the call of Christ, especially as mediated through St. Francis. She saw her brothers and sisters in need and responded.

Revelation 3:1–6,14–22 or 1 John 3:14–18
Psalm 15:2–3a,3bc–4ab,5 or 34:2–3,4–5,6–7,8–9,10–11
Luke 19:1–10 or 6:27–38

"A nobleman went off to a distant country to obtain the kingship for himself and then to return. He called ten of his servants and gave them ten gold coins and told them, 'Engage in trade with these until I return.'"
—LUKE 19:12–13

This parable that Jesus tells in Luke is similar to what we know as the Parable of the Talents in the Gospel of Matthew. We know that the "talents" in Jesus' parable refer to currency, not abilities, but that association can still shape our response to this story. Don't waste my gifts and talents, I'm told. Perhaps. But I also have to be careful that I don't use my discernment of gifts as an excuse to ignore other people's tough, unglamorous needs in the present moment. The master has instructed us to engage with the world until he returns. Our currency? His love and grace, to be shared in the give and take of ordinary, everyday life.

Revelation 4:1–11 or Acts 28:11–16,30–31
Psalm 150:1b–2,3–4,5–6 or 98:1,2–3ab,3cd–4,5–6
Luke 19:11–28 or Matthew 14:22–33

NOVEMBER 19

*As Jesus drew near Jerusalem, he saw the city and wept over it, saying,
"If this day you only knew what makes for peace—but now it is hidden
from your eyes."*
—LUKE 19:41–42

We often take "progress" for granted. But I wonder: Is our
modern sense of progress—the idea that human history is a
steady, inexorable march to human betterment—really true?
And does it fit with the Christian worldview? In these last
days of Ordinary Time, we hear more and more about
creation's purpose and direction. Yes, we are progressing
toward redemption and fulfillment in Christ, who gathers us.
But human beings still sin; we still exploit one another (albeit
with cleaner water and more efficient technology than ever
before). But don't Jesus' words still ring true? That peace for
which we yearn seems just beyond our seeing.

Revelation 5:1–10
Psalm 149:1b–2,3–4,5–6a,9b
Luke 19:41–44

NOVEMBER 20

Jesus entered the temple area and proceeded to drive out those who were selling things, saying to them, "It is written, My house shall be a house of prayer, but you have made it a den of thieves."
—LUKE 19:45–46

When touring Japan, we visited many Buddhist and Shinto spiritual sites. The way to each of them was lined with shops and restaurants, right up to the gate and even beyond. That mix of commerce and spirituality is universal, it seems, and hard to resist. People seek peace and search for answers, so the canny businessperson takes advantage of that dependable market. I can cluck in disapproval, or I can instead turn it around and reflect on the ways that I regard my spiritual life as a way to gain or profit rather than to serve.

Revelation 10:8–11
Psalm 119:14,24,72,103,111,131
Luke 19:45–48

NOVEMBER 21

• THE PRESENTATION OF THE BLESSED VIRGIN MARY •

O God, I will sing a new song to you;
with a ten-stringed lyre I will chant your praise.
—PSALM 144:9

It is one thing to praise God when life is going my way and I am filled with positive feelings. But what about when I'm suffering, or when those I love are suffering? Is my prayer life preparing me for the moments when I'm challenged, when life has turned upside down, to still lift my voice in praise and gratitude?

Revelation 11:4–12
Psalm 144:1b,2,9–10
Luke 20:27–40

Then the king will say to those on his right, "Come, you who are blessed by my Father. Inherit the kingdom prepared for you from the foundation of the world. For I was hungry and you gave me food, I was thirsty and you gave me drink, a stranger and you welcomed me, naked and you clothed me, ill and you cared for me, in prison and you visited me."
—MATTHEW 25:34–36

Think about the monarchs who've ruled over other human beings throughout history. Consider what they demand of their subjects: money, land, labor, loyalty oaths, and even worship. What does our King expect? He rules over heaven and earth. We are beholden to him for our lives, and what does he ask in return? That we serve him, through serving others first.

Ezekiel 34:11–12,15–17
Psalm 23:1–2,2–3,5–6
1 Corinthians 15:20–26,28
Matthew 25:31–46

• ST. CLEMENT I, POPE AND MARTYR • ST. COLUMBAN, ABBOT • BLESSED
MIGUEL AGUSTÍN PRO, PRIEST AND MARTYR •

*[Jesus] said, "I tell you truly, this poor widow put in more than all the
rest; for those others have all made offerings from their surplus wealth,
but she, from her poverty, has offered her whole livelihood."*
—LUKE 21:3–4

Why hold back? Why dip into my surplus—of time, money,
and other resources—and not, as the widow does, give all
from my poverty? I suppose it all comes down to trust. I can
trust all the stuff and time and energy I'm holding on to, or I
can lean fully on God's power to care for me when I've taken
that deep breath and given it all to him.

Revelation 14:1–3,4b–5
Psalm 24:1bc–2,3–4ab,5–6
Luke 21:1–4

Jesus said, "All that you see here—the days will come when there will not be left a stone upon another stone that will not be thrown down."
—LUKE 21:6

There's a store here in Alabama called Unclaimed Baggage, a business built on reselling lost luggage and the paraphernalia passengers leave behind on planes. I walked into the place and was immediately deeply conscious of how everything that surrounded me—every piece of clothing, every laptop, every pair of shoes—represented something more than the sum of its parts. They represented anger, frustration, loss, and disruption. There's also a bigger story that all this stuff is a part of, the story that Jesus alludes to here. That's the story of a material world that can shine with meaning, but in the end is, indeed, passing away.

Revelation 14:14–19
Psalm 96:10,11–12,13
Luke 21:5–11

NOVEMBER 25

• ST. CATHERINE OF ALEXANDRIA, VIRGIN AND MARTYR •

You will even be handed over by parents, brothers, relatives, and friends,
and they will put some of you to death. You will be hated by all because
of my name, but not a hair on your head will be destroyed. By your
perseverance you will secure your lives.

—LUKE 21:16–19

Father James Coyle, pastor of the cathedral in Birmingham,
Alabama, was sitting on the rectory porch on an August
evening in 1921, when he was shot and killed. The murderer
was the Methodist-minister father of a young woman whom,
earlier in the day, Father Coyle had secretly married to a
Puerto Rican man. Father Coyle is one of millions who have
suffered for their faith, but consider the paradox Jesus lays
out here: put to death . . . but not a hair destroyed. We trust
in the One who is stronger than death.

Revelation 15:1–4
Psalm 98:1,2–3ab,7–8,9
Luke 21:12–19

NOVEMBER 26

• THANKSGIVING DAY •

*I give thanks to my God always on your account for the grace of God
bestowed on you in Christ Jesus, that in him you were enriched
in every way.*
—1 CORINTHIANS 1:4–5

I am an only child, and it took me a while to figure out that
the natural family dynamic of that situation led to a
subconscious assumption that I am (or should be) the center
of everyone's world. Weird, but also pretty deeply engrained
in my psyche, and it's not a good thing. Sometimes we are
tempted to shrug about those mysteriously deep aspects of
personality and say, "That's just the way I am." I'm thankful
that in Christ I've been given a greater gift—to change, to
move beyond even what seems unchangeable, and be
enriched by his grace to conform to him.

Revelation 18:1–2,21–23; 19:1–3,9a
Psalm 100:1b–2,3,4,5
Luke 21:20–28

PROPER MASS IN
THANKSGIVING TO GOD:
1 Kings 8:55–61
1 Corinthians 1:3–9
1 Chronicles 29:10bc,11,12
Matthew 7:7–11
Other readings may be selected.

NOVEMBER 27

> *Then I saw a new heaven and a new earth. The former heaven and the*
> *former earth had passed away, and the sea was no more. I also saw the*
> *holy city, a new Jerusalem, coming down out of heaven from God,*
> *prepared as a bride adorned for her husband.*
> —REVELATION 21:1–2

It's a glorious vision, to be sure. But what has preceded it? War, persecution, and suffering: a great battle. John's vision is vivid and extreme but is still recognizable to us in the midst of our own battles with darkness. In hope, we gather for a glimpse of the new earth, even here on the old earth. As we gather in communion with one another and with him, we find hope in the celebration, and we take joy in the feast.

Revelation 20:1–4,11—21:2
Psalm 84:3,4,5–6a,8a
Luke 21:29–33

NOVEMBER 28

Come, let us sing joyfully to the LORD;
let us acclaim the Rock of our salvation.
—PSALM 95:1

My friend's teenage son was concerned. It was a faith crisis of sorts. As a teen in a Catholic school participating in youth ministry events, he was convinced that he was lacking in faith. Why? Because everything he attended emphasized emotional responses. He had come to assume that having faith meant crying, singing in a certain way, or just feeling a kind of high. It took some time, but he eventually came to understand that everyone is different and that faith—trust, belief in, and love of the Lord—can be expressed and even felt in varied ways. We all sing to the Lord, some just more quietly than others.

Revelation 22:1–7
Psalm 95:1–2,3–5,6–7ab
Luke 21:34–36

"Watch, therefore; you do not know when the lord of the house is coming, whether in the evening, or at midnight, or at cockcrow, or in the morning. May he not come suddenly and find you sleeping. What I say to you, I say to all: 'Watch!'"

—MARK 13:35–37

There are nights in which this warning is not exactly a challenge for me: those nights in which I literally can't sleep. Stress builds because, well, I can't sleep—so I end up tense and angry. After years of battling this, I decided on a different approach. Instead of focusing on my own frustration, I'd use the moment. Is there a reason I'm awake? Is there something I'm supposed to be noticing in these dark, silent hours? What might become clear to me here in the silence that's hidden from me in the noisy, busy light of day?

Isaiah 63:16b–17,19b; 64:2–7
Psalm 80:2–3,15–16,18–19
1 Corinthians 1:3–9
Mark 13:33–37

As Jesus was walking by the Sea of Galilee, he saw two brothers, Simon who is called Peter, and his brother Andrew, casting a net into the sea; they were fishermen. He said to them, "Come after me, and I will make you fishers of men." At once they left their nets and followed him.
—MATTHEW 4:18–20

During Advent we are surrounded by the familiar: the decor, the prayers, the devotional practices, and simply the rhythm of the days leading up to Christmas. But paradoxically, all this familiarity is about something surprising and strange. It is about God incarnate, the Lord of the universe, born to a woman, growing up in a nowhere village in a backwater of the Roman Empire—and being invited, one fine ordinary day in the midst of our everyday tasks, to change our lives and follow him.

Romans 10:9–18
Psalm 19:8,9,10,11
Matthew 4:18–22

DECEMBER 1

There shall be no harm or ruin on all my holy mountain;
for the earth shall be filled with knowledge of the LORD,
as water covers the sea.
—ISAIAH 11:9

Les Invalides is the massive former military hospital in Paris
that now houses the over-the-top tomb of Napoleon and
other leaders, as well as the largest collection of armor and
weaponry I've ever seen. Impressive, but depressing. Yes, war
can be just and serve to defend the innocent, but still. All this
human ingenuity, creativity, and attention to detail and even
beauty (much of it was quite ornately made), at the service of
violence and worldly power. I trust in the Lord's promise that
in his time, according to his purpose for us, peace will reign,
and beauty will serve only life, not death.

Isaiah 11:1–10
Psalm 72:1–2,7–8,12–13,17
Luke 10:21–24

Jesus summoned his disciples and said, "My heart is moved with pity for the crowd, for they have been with me now for three days and have nothing to eat."
—MATTHEW 15:32

Does God really care? Years ago I had a spiritual breakthrough of sorts when I realized that I was operating out of some deeply held, barely conscious assumption that God probably didn't really care about me. A belief that my stumbles and missteps were a matter of—oh, I don't know—maybe even a sort of cosmic amusement at my expense. What a relief to hear Jesus' words! What a welcome change to really understand that those assumptions weren't true. The Lord created me for a reason, loves me, and sees my struggle, not from a distance but from a heart moved with pity.

Isaiah 25:6–10a
Psalm 23:1–3a,3b–4,5,6
Matthew 15:29–37

Jesus said to his disciples: "Not everyone who says to me, 'Lord, Lord,'
will enter the Kingdom of heaven, but only the one who does the will of
my Father in heaven."

—MATTHEW 7:21

During Advent we are preparing our hearts for the Word
made flesh, for God incarnate. How does this change the
world? How does it change me? The diverse saints of Advent
point the way. St. Lucy, St. Nicholas, St. Juan Diego,
St. John of the Cross, and today's St. Francis Xavier show us
what it means to respond to the Incarnation not just with
words but also with actions. As Pope Benedict XVI said in a
General Audience address of 2010: "Truly, dear friends, the
saints are the best interpreters of the Bible. As they incarnate
the Word of God in their own lives, they make it more
captivating than ever, so that it really speaks to us."

Isaiah 26:1–6
Psalm 118:1,8–9,19–21,25–27a
Matthew 7:21,24–27

Friday

DECEMBER 4

> *Then he touched their eyes and said, "Let it be done for you*
> *according to your faith."*
> —MATTHEW 9:29

It is so fitting to remember St. John Damascene during these
preparation days for Christmas. He was, after all, the
eighth-century monastic saint who defended the veneration
of images against the challenges of iconoclasts. His
argument, from his discourse *The Orthodox Faith*, rests on the
Incarnation: "And so the Son of God, while still remaining in
the form of God, lowered the skies and descended . . . to his
servants, . . . achieving the newest thing of all, the only thing
really new under the sun, through which he manifested the
infinite power of God." God created the material world.
God's power moves through matter—most powerfully
through the touch of Jesus Christ, the image of the
invisible God.

Isaiah 29:17–24
Psalm 27:1,4,13–14
Matthew 9:27–31

While from behind, a voice shall sound in your ears:
"This is the way, walk in it,"
when you would turn to the right or the left.
—ISAIAH 30:21

Traveling in Europe, I could speak and understand just enough French or Italian to get by, if I was certain of the context. What threw me, however, were times when another person standing next to me in line would toss off a comment in passing, as people do. Without context, their words were just noise. Context is important in being able to hear God's Word to me as well. If the context in which I live my life is primarily shaped by the language of the world, will I be able to recognize and understand the Lord's voice when he speaks?

Isaiah 30:19–21,23–26
Psalm 147:1–2,3–4,5–6
Matthew 9:35—10:1,5a,6–8

Sunday

DECEMBER 6

• SECOND SUNDAY OF ADVENT •

*Comfort, give comfort to my people,
says your God.*
—ISAIAH 40:1

As the mother of five, as a friend, as a person who has
experienced the loss of both parents and a husband, I have
some experience with giving and receiving comfort. How do
we give comfort? It can be so awkward sometimes. We
usually think, *I just don't know what to say.* Well, once you are
on the receiving end for long enough and have gotten over
the self-consciousness of youth, you know about one
important thing: presence. That's it. Thoughtful, loving,
attentive presence. Which is exactly the comfort we're
promised by the Lord who loves us and knows our suffering:
his real presence, with us in the midst of it all.

Isaiah 40:1–5,9–11
Psalm 85:9–10,11–12,13–14
2 Peter 3:8–14
Mark 1:1–8

DECEMBER 7

• ST. AMBROSE, BISHOP AND DOCTOR OF THE CHURCH •

But not finding a way to bring him in because of the crowd, they went up on the roof and lowered him on the stretcher through the tiles into the middle in front of Jesus.

—LUKE 5:19

Is there someone I know who is in need? What can I do today to help that person; what steps can I take, no matter how unexpected or outside the box, to bring him or her into the presence of Jesus' healing, merciful touch?

Isaiah 35:1–10
Psalm 85:9ab,10,11–12,13–14
Luke 5:17–26

DECEMBER 8

• THE IMMACULATE CONCEPTION OF THE BLESSED VIRGIN MARY
(PATRONAL FEASTDAY OF THE UNITED STATES OF AMERICA) •

*All the ends of the earth have seen
the salvation by our God.*
—PSALM 98:3

Every year on the feast of the Immaculate Conception, my
thoughts turn to the Monkees. You know, the 1960s
made-for-television band? Why on earth? Well, on one of their
Christmas specials, they offered a lovely, charming a cappella
version of a Spanish Renaissance tune called "Riu, Riu Chiu." In
English, it begins, "River, roaring river, guard our homes in
safety, God has kept the black wolf from our lamb, our Lady."
It's about today's feast: God's grace protecting Mary from sin
from conception. And flowing from that grace was the gift of
Jesus, the Word made flesh. From eternity, to the girl in
Nazareth, to sixteenth-century Spain, to 1960s pop music, to
me, clicking on a link on my computer today. Indeed, all the
ends of the earth have seen the salvation by our God.

Genesis 3:9–15,20
Psalm 98:1,2–3ab,3cd–4
Ephesians 1:3–6,11–12
Luke 1:26–38

DECEMBER 9

• ST. JUAN DIEGO CUAUHTLATOATZIN •

Do you not know
or have you not heard? . . .
He gives strength to the fainting;
for the weak he makes vigor abound.
—ISAIAH 40:28–29

This is the season. It's the season when images of light and warmth and songs about love for a child, peace, and joy permeate even this most secular culture. Hearts might be a little more open, the seeker might be a bit more intentional, ready to stop drifting, hungry for solid food. It's the season that I pray my witness might be part of that tapestry, offering hope in some way to those who are weary of depending on themselves, of carrying the burden of loneliness. We have good news: Have you not heard? You're not alone. He has come. Because he loves you. Yes, you.

Isaiah 40:25–31
Psalm 103:1–2,3–4,8,10
Matthew 11:28–30

DECEMBER 10

I am the LORD, your God,
who grasp your right hand;
It is I who say to you, "Fear not,
I will help you."
—ISAIAH 41:13

God took on flesh, not in another world but in this world—our world. A world of lost opportunities and mistakes rooted, at times, in what we experienced as children, regrets and memories that can sometimes loom large around this time of year. Childhood still calls, though, but of a different sort. Another Child—in the flesh, fully alive, taking our hand—invites us to trust not in a regrettable past but in a joyous present of reconciling peace, strong and without fear.

Isaiah 41:13–20
Psalm 145:1,9,10–11,12–13ab
Matthew 11:11–15

I, the LORD, your God,
teach you what is for your good,
and lead you on the way you should go.
—ISAIAH 48:17

During the second week of Advent, our parish celebrated what is called a Rorate Mass. The name comes from the Latin of the first two words of the Introit prayer: *Rorate, Caeli*—"Drop down dew, O heavens." The Mass, in honor of the Blessed Virgin, begins at dawn. Ours was at 6:15 a.m. And I made it! The beauty of the liturgy is that it is celebrated in the dark in candlelight, but by the time Mass ends, dawn has broken. You walk into the church in the darkness, but when you leave, you're walking into the light. It's a microcosm of the Advent journey and the journey of faith for all of us. Out of darkness, the Lord leads us to the light of his love.

Isaiah 48:17–19
Psalm 1:1–2,3,4, 6
Matthew 11:16–19

*Silence, all mankind, in the presence of the LORD! For he stirs forth from
his holy dwelling!*
—ZECHARIAH 2:17

The experience of seeing the tilma of Our Lady of
Guadalupe was not what I expected. We tumbled out of our
taxi on the busy street, went through a door on the ground
floor of the basilica, walked through a short hallway, stepped
onto a moving walkway, looked up—and there she was. I
thought there would be more of a buildup, that the approach
would be more worshipful and majestic. The basilica is lovely
and serene, but that unexpectedly hurried first view surprised
me. But then, isn't that fitting, since so much about this
young girl, the mother of the Savior stirring forth, the bearer
of Good News to this continent, is a surprise?

Zechariah 2:14–17 or Revelation 11:19a; 12:1–6a,10ab
Judith 13:18bcde,19
Luke 1:26–38 or 1:39–47

Brothers and sisters: Rejoice always. Pray without ceasing. In all circumstances give thanks, for this is the will of God for you in Christ Jesus.
—1 THESSALONIANS 5:16–18

Always? In all circumstances? How is that done? It is possible. You've probably passed through great pain of one sort or another. You've suffered. But still, you've found a way to rejoice and give thanks. In times when it seems difficult or impossible, in times when Paul's words seem like an unreachable ideal and the joy of this season like a mockery, think back to those moments of prayerful joy. In the midst of sadness in the past, you've found joy. Let Jesus lead you to that place again.

Isaiah 61:1–2a,10–11
Luke 1:46–48,49–50,53–54
1 Thessalonians 5:16–24
John 1:6–8,19–28

Guide me in your truth and teach me,
for you are my God my savior.
—PSALM 25:5

One spring morning, a small bird entered our open front
door. We discovered it on the sill of the front picture
window, flinging itself against it, fruitlessly beating its wings.
From the creature's view, the way was clear to the limitless
sky and perhaps even the tree branches of home. What was
this barrier? I, too, can see the promise of that home for
which I was so lovingly and intentionally created. It's time to
take stock of my own shortsightedness and let the Lord
lower the barriers I've constructed, to open myself to his
truth and let him guide me.

Numbers 24:2–7,15–17a
Psalm 25:4–5ab,6,7bc,8–9
Matthew 21:23–27

DECEMBER 15

"A man had two sons. He came to the first and said, 'Son, go out and work in the vineyard today.' The son said in reply, 'I will not,' but afterwards he changed his mind and went."
—MATTHEW 21:28–31

Charles de Foucauld grew to adulthood far from Christ. After serving in the military and spending years as a student of the peoples of northern Africa, Charles started responding to the voice of Christ calling him. He gave himself over to living out the gospel in a radical way, welcoming and serving people from all backgrounds. His Prayer of Abandonment embodies his radical yes to God after years of saying no: "Father, I abandon myself into your hands; do with me what you will. Whatever you may do, I thank you: I am ready for all, I accept all."

Zephaniah 3:1–2,9–13
Psalm 34:2–3,6–7,17–18,19,23
Matthew 21:28–32

DECEMBER 16

I am the LORD, there is no other;
I form the light, and create the darkness,
I make well-being and create woe;
I, the LORD, do all these things.
—ISAIAH 45:6b–7

One year in Germany I picked up a different sort of Advent candle. It's a single thick taper that's decorated from top to bottom with various designs as well as a series of numbers, like a ruler. That burning candle takes you through the days of Advent one by one. This single candle burns as a reminder of an Advent paradox: the Incarnation reveals how God's light shines through Creation to overcome the darkness and meet us where we are in this passing world; at the same time it points us toward what is to come, more that will never, ever melt away.

Isaiah 45:6b–8,18,21c–25
Psalm 85:9ab and 10,11–12,13–14
Luke 7:18b–23

Thursday
DECEMBER 17

Salmon the father of Boaz, whose mother was Rahab. Boaz became the
father of Obed, whose mother was Ruth. Obed became the father of
Jesse, Jesse the father of David the king.
—MATTHEW 1:5–6

Today we begin the "O Antiphons" that highlight Jesus'
ancient, Old Testament-rooted Messianic titles. They are
prayed during evening prayer and also as the verse in the
Gospel Acclamation for Mass. The first is a prayer asking the
Lord as Wisdom to continue to guide us. This, along with
today's Gospel reading that digs deeply into Jesus' roots in
the varied, diverse course of human history, reminds us of the
great, rich story that we are a part of. We are not alone but
are walking with a great family, with the Lord right here to
guide us in wisdom.

Genesis 49:2,8–10
Psalm 72:1–2,3–4ab,7–8,17
Matthew 1:1–17

"Joseph, son of David, do not be afraid to take Mary your wife into your home. For it is through the Holy Spirit that this child has been conceived in her. She will bear a son and you are to name him Jesus, because he will save his people from their sins."

—MATTHEW 1:20–21

How often do we search for God "out there," when all the time the Lord is right here with us? Of course, having faith in his presence doesn't always translate into feeling that presence. Ask St. Teresa of Calcutta, one of such deep faith who suffered, we now know, times of profound spiritual desolation and dryness. But acknowledging the complexity and the risk, we can step forward in faith and open ourselves to the Lord's presence. And when we discern the Lord's will—as Joseph did—we will trust and follow.

Jeremiah 23:5–8
Psalm 72:1–2,12–13,18–19
Matthew 1:18–25

DECEMBER 19

"'You will conceive and bear a son . . . for this boy is to be consecrated to God from the womb.'"
—JUDGES 13:7

This year my oldest son will be thirty-eight years old and my youngest will be sixteen, with a few kids in between. If I have learned anything in all those decades of parenting, it is the hard but beautiful lesson that other human beings don't belong to us—they belong to God. They are not put here on earth to reflect us, compensate for us, or be used by us. They are on their own journey, created by God, on their way to him, a journey that calls me to respect and support them, and leads me to grateful prayer for their lives.

Judges 13:2–7,24–25a
Psalm 71:3–4a,5–6ab,16–17
Luke 1:5–25

DECEMBER 20

• FOURTH SUNDAY OF ADVENT •

*Brothers and sisters: To him who can strengthen you, according to my
gospel and the proclamation of Jesus Christ, according to the revelation
of the mystery kept secret for long ages . . . to the only wise God, through
Jesus Christ be glory forever and ever. Amen.*
—ROMANS 16:25,27

We might wonder why God has saved us in this strange,
specific way. Why not a more general revelation wafting
itself over humanity like a mist? But here's the paradox: It's
those puzzling specifics that in the end are so revelatory. The
idea of a Savior is great, but the fact of a Savior born to a
young woman in a village—it brings me out of myself. No
matter what I expect, He is who he is, in that time and that
place, and paradoxically, for all time and all places. Forever.

2 Samuel 7:1–5,8b–12,14a,16
Psalm 89:2–3,4–5,27,29 (2a)
Romans 16:25–27
Luke 1:26–38

Monday

DECEMBER 21

• ST. PETER CANISIUS, PRIEST AND DOCTOR OF THE CHURCH •

"For at the moment the sound of your greeting reached my ears, the infant in my womb leaped for joy."
—LUKE 1:44

Christmas is a season of visiting and socializing and serving one another. All of this activity can be draining, and keeping focus might be a struggle. It certainly is for my introverted self. *How can I focus on Jesus with all of these other people around?* I wonder. It helps to remember this special moment between Elizabeth and Mary (and John and Jesus). It reminds me that by simply and genuinely welcoming another, I welcome Christ.

Song of Songs 2:8–14 or Zephaniah 3:14–18a
Psalm 33:2–3,11–12,20–21
Luke 1:39–45

Tuesday

DECEMBER 22

Mary said:
"My soul proclaims the greatness of the Lord;
my spirit rejoices in God my savior."
—LUKE 1:46–47

At the end of a journey in the midst of surprising events, Mary turned to the Lord and gave praise and thanks. Today or tomorrow, in a completely unexpected place—a place and time in which you've never thought to pray before—take a moment and give thanks.

1 Samuel 1:24–28
1 Samuel 2:1,4–5,6–7,8abcd
Luke 1:46–56

When the time arrived for Elizabeth to have her child she gave birth to a son. Her neighbors and relatives heard that the Lord had shown his great mercy toward her, and they rejoiced with her.
—LUKE 1:57–58

My oldest son was living in New York City. I said, "I've never experienced Christmas in the City. Let's go!" So we did, and, well, the best I can say is (no offense)—been there, done that. Sure, it was pretty, but the people! What a mad crush of humanity, especially around Rockefeller Center and on Fifth Avenue. I was tempted to be annoyed and sniff, "Do you people even get Christmas? Or is this just an excuse to party and spend?" But what is that but my pride? No matter how faint the Good News may be, they had heard something—and had gathered to rejoice.

Malachi 3:1–4,23–24
Psalm 25:4–5ab,8–9,10,14
Luke 1:57–66

DECEMBER 24

In the tender compassion of our God
the dawn from on high shall break upon us,
to shine on those who dwell in darkness and the shadow of death,
and guide our feet into the way of peace.
—LUKE 1:78–79

This time of year can be so difficult for so many people. Images of warm family life and high expectations have the power to deepen our emotions as we cope with loss, brokenness, and anxiety. Which is, of course, exactly why the Lord has come: to meet us, not in an ideal world or a fantasy but in the very real place where we live, marked by both light and shadows, joy and sadness. He has come to shower us right there with his tender compassion.

2 Samuel 7:1–5,8b–12,14a,16
Psalm 89:2–3,4–5,27,29
Luke 1:67–79

Friday

DECEMBER 25

• THE NATIVITY OF THE LORD (CHRISTMAS) •

*Then the shepherds returned, glorifying and praising God for all they
had heard and seen, just as it had been told to them.*

—LUKE 2:20

One of my favorite children's Christmas books is *Can It Be
True?* by Susan Hill, inspired by Thomas Hardy's poem
"Oxen." In it, all earth's battling creatures sense a change.
"Can it be true? Can it be true?" is the constant refrain. Can it
really be true that we don't have to live like this? That there
is another way? On each page, former enemies inch closer to
Bethlehem and discover, yes, "It is true! It is true!
And knelt down."

VIGIL:
Isaiah 62:1–5
Psalm 89:4–5,16–17,27,29 (2a)
Acts 13:16–17,22–25
Matthew 1:1–25 or 1:18–25

DAWN:
Isaiah 62:11–12
Psalm 97:1,6,11–12
Titus 3:4–7
Luke 2:15–20

NIGHT:
Isaiah 9:1–6
Psalm 96:1–2,2–3,11–12,13
Titus 2:11–14
Luke 2:1–14

DAY:
Isaiah 52:7–10
Psalm 98:1,2–3,3–4,5–6 (3c)
Hebrews 1:1–6
John 1:1–18 or 1:1–5,9–14

DECEMBER 26

• ST. STEPHEN, THE FIRST MARTYR •

You are my rock and my fortress;
for your name's sake you will lead and guide me.
—PSALM 31:4

I've long had this intuition that our greatest weaknesses are
also our greatest strengths, and vice versa. The willful,
stubborn child could probably be a strong leader. The child
whose sensitivity seems to indicate fragility might become a
sympathetic listener. I have, shall we say, a pretty relaxed
attitude toward much of life. Perhaps I shouldn't indulge that
tendency all the time. Yet at times, might an attitude some
people perceive as a weakness offer a welcome moment of
calm? Rooted in the Lord as my rock, I'm challenged to let
him guide me in turning every part of my personality, no
matter how it's seen by the outside world, over to him.

Acts 6:8–10; 7:54–59
Psalm 31:3cd–4,6,8ab,16bc,17
Matthew 10:17–22

DECEMBER 27

[S]he gave thanks to God and spoke about the child to all who were
awaiting the redemption of Jerusalem.
—LUKE 2:38

I took my grandson out to a bookstore to buy a gift for his dad, my son. I asked him what kind of book he thought his dad would like. "Something about elephants," he insisted. Long ago, when that dad was a little boy, his Mother's Day gift to me was a flowerpot decorated with Batman symbols. When we give gifts, of course we want to think of the other person's interests and needs. But isn't it true our gifts also express something about who we are? And the perfect gift—the gift of Jesus—is wrapped up into both: everything he is and all that we need.

Genesis 15:1–6; 21:1–3 or Sirach 3:2–6,12–14
Psalm 105:1–2,3–4,5–6,8–9 (7a,8a) or 128:1–2,3,4–5
Hebrews 11:8,11–12,17–19 or Colossians 3:12–21 or 3:12–17
Luke 2:22–40 or 2:22,39–40

Monday

DECEMBER 28

• THE HOLY INNOCENTS, MARTYRS •

*When Herod realized that he had been deceived by the magi, he became
furious. He ordered the massacre of all the boys in Bethlehem and its
vicinity two years old and under, in accordance with the time he had
ascertained from the magi.*
—MATTHEW 2:16

The cries of the Holy Innocents echo through the centuries,
but not from the past. The innocent still suffer. The spiritual
writer Caryll Houselander writes about the Holy Innocents
in her book *The Passion of the Infant Christ*: "Herod ordered the
children to be killed because he was afraid that any one of
them might be Christ. Any child might be Christ! The fear of
Herod is the fear of every tyrant, the hope of every
Christian, and the most significant fact in the modern world."

1 John 1:5—2:2
Psalm 124:2–3,4–5,7b–8
Matthew 2:13–18

DECEMBER 29

• ST. THOMAS BECKET, BISHOP AND MARTYR •

"Lord, now let your servant go in peace;
your word has been fulfilled:
my own eyes have seen the salvation."
—LUKE 2:29–30

I read these words of Simeon, and I always remember a night over ten years ago. It was the Feast of the Presentation. Our family was praying evening prayer. Simeon's prayer, the *Nunc Dimittis*, is always part of night prayer anyway, but it had more meaning on the celebration of this moment in Jesus' life. We prayed it together—my husband, the three children at home, and I. The very next morning, Mike suffered a heart attack and died. I've always taken comfort in that fact: that the last words I remember in my husband's voice were the words of a prayer of trust. Jesus is with us. We can go on and finish the journey in peace.

1 John 2:3–11
Psalm 96:1–2a,2b–3,5b–6
Luke 2:22–35

DECEMBER 30

*The child grew and became strong, filled with wisdom; and the favor of
God was upon him.*
—LUKE 2:40

When I first began traveling in a serious way, I was a single
parent accompanied by my two younger sons. I hauled them
all over, and it was fun. There were times, though, I would
muse over what it would be like to travel alone. You'd think
I'd be happy about the possibility of doing what I wanted.
But the vision actually saddened me. Partly because I do
enjoy their company, but also because seeing the world
through their eyes expands mine. Come to think of it, at
home or on the road, I journey with another Child
companion. How different the world looks through his eyes
of wisdom, of understanding, of mercy. Through him I see
how precious is each person I meet and how hope-filled is
the road ahead.

1 John 2:12–17
Psalm 96:7–8a,8b–9,10
Luke 2:36–40

The LORD comes,
he comes to rule the earth.
—PSALM 96:13

Thank you, Lord. Thank you for another year of life. Thank you for each moment of each day. Thank you for the coming time, whatever it holds. May I remember always that you rule the earth, you are the loving Lord of my life, and in you, I need not fear anything that is to come.

1 John 2:18–21
Psalm 96:1–2,11–12,13
John 1:1–18

ABOUT THE AUTHOR

Amy Welborn is the author of *A Catholic Woman's Book of Days* and several titles in the Loyola Kids series, most recently *Loyola Kids Book of Catholic Signs & Symbols*. A former catechetical leader, she is passionate about helping readers live their faith with confidence and joy.